Creative Learning for the Information Age

Creative Learning for the Information Age

How Classrooms Can Better Prepare Students (2nd Edition)

Lyn Lesch

ROWMAN & LITTLEFIELD
Lanham • Boulder • New York • Toronto • Plymouth, UK

Published by Rowman & Littlefield
4501 Forbes Boulevard, Suite 200, Lanham, Maryland 20706
www.rowman.com

10 Thornbury Road, Plymouth PL6 7PP, United Kingdom

British Library Cataloguing in Publication Information Available

Library of Congress Cataloging-in-Publication Data

Lesch, Lyn, 1948-
Creative learning for the information age : how classrooms can better prepare students / Lyn Lesch. -- Second edition.
p. cm.
Rev. ed. of: How to prepare students for the information age and global marketplace.
Includes bibliographical references.
ISBN 978-1-61048-944-7 (cloth : alk. paper) -- ISBN 978-1-61048-945-4 (pbk. : alk. paper) -- ISBN 978-1-61048-946-1 (electronic)
1. Learning. 2. Education--Philosophy. 3. Creative ability. 4. Creative thinking. 5. Education--Effect of technological innovations on. I. Lesch, Lyn, 1948- How to prepare students for the information age and global marketplace. II. Title.
LB1060.L485 2014
370.15'23--dc23
2014008576

♾™ The paper used in this publication meets the minimum requirements of American National Standard for Information Sciences Permanence of Paper for Printed Library Materials, ANSI/NISO Z39.48-1992.

Printed in the United States of America

For Chip and Sheryl

Contents

Introduction   1

1   A New Paradigm   5

2   Barriers to Success   17

3   New Skills for a New Time   31

4   Accountability and Initiative   43

5   A Proper Structure   57

6   Teacher and Student   69

7   The World Outside of School   79

8   The Inner Lives of Children in the Digital Age   91

9   A Distracted Awareness and Creativity   105

10   The Future of Schooling   115

Bibliography   121

About the Author   125

Introduction

During the twelve years the alternative school of which I was founder and director, The Children's School of Evanston, Illinois, was in existence, I was able to maintain a particular vision of what creative learning might entail. Because the students at our school, who were between the ages of six and fourteen, were not subject to standardized test scores, and were not taught according to any sort of preplanned curriculum that they didn't have a hand in creating, I was able to develop a certain unique perspective on the possibilities for approaching various subject areas and learning progressions that I would not have had if the students' curricula had been more predetermined.

In other words, because the staff at our school was not beholden to either a state-mandated curriculum or the sort of preconceived approaches employed in other private schools, such as the Montessori or Waldorf schools, we were often able to experiment with developing certain original approaches, those which were in conjunction with the students' own interests and tendencies, to various areas of learning.

Out of that experience, one of the things I learned, which leads toward the subject of this book, was how to facilitate more creative learning for students in their formative years by setting up lessons in a manner in which young people learn how to make their own connections between relevant information and knowledge in apprehending various subject matters, rather than being given those connections in advance.

That is, rather than simply giving students knowledge and information at the beginning of a lesson and then expecting them to learn it in a predetermined manner, if one instead introduces the lesson in a way that actually gives students the latitude to acquire that knowledge and information more indirectly by making significant connections for themselves, they will be able to employ a more creative approach as they learn.

Of course, a developing awareness of the significance of doing this, and how to in fact actually do it were things that did not come quickly or easily. Initially, during the school's early years, it often seemed that if we wished students to learn in a more creative manner, it was enough to simply introduce creative materials and ideas into lessons. Only later did we comprehend more fully that it was the design of the lessons themselves, as well as the overall learning environment in which they originated, which in fact facilitated more creative learning.

Over time, we learned how to present students with learning activities in a manner that permitted them to perceive certain relationships and make relevant connections for themselves, rather than simply giving these to them in advance in the form of knowledge or information to be acquired. In fact, more and more I found myself attempting to present subject matter to students almost in the form of interesting riddles to be solved, rather than teaching it to them in a more direct manner.

Out of this, I began to learn that if one wishes to engender truly creative learning in students in their formative years, it is not enough to simply teach them how to perceive significant patterns or connections or to design lessons that will allow this to occur, although both of these things are of course extremely important. One must also make the sort of significant structural changes in one's school or classroom that will permit more creative approaches to learning to genuinely take place.

Since the time when my school closed in 2003, and the time when my last book on the subject of students in their formative years learning more creatively in preparation for the information age that they will soon inherit appeared in 2008, there have been a number of profound changes taking place in the digital world that we all now increasingly inhabit—changes that make it more necessary than ever that classroom structures in schools change in order to prepare students to learn more effectively in preparation for this new age they will soon enter as adults.

For one, with the emergence of websites like Facebook and Twitter, as well as the seemingly endless amount of text messaging in which people are now involved, the ability that people now have to connect with one another through social media has now become a primary means of communication throughout the world. Hence, those with creative ideas in any particular field of endeavor are able to collaborate with others who have similar interests at a rate of speed that just several years ago would have been unimaginable.

Another significant change that has occurred is that as digital technology becomes increasingly more user friendly and more accessible to everyone, it has become easier for teachers to incorporate these new technologies directly into the structure of classroom learning environments in ways that allow for greater creativity by the students who employ them. This occurs from the secondary school down through even the kindergarten level.

Yet, as much as anything, with the advent of the Internet, the nature of knowledge itself in any number of different areas of human endeavor appears to be changing at an ever-increasing rate of speed. That is, as experts in different fields are able to connect with each other much more quickly and more completely than was previously thought possible, they are able to rapidly transform their expertise into something new—or else imagine a whole range of applications for their expertise—at a rate of change that might have shocked even Alvin Toffler when he wrote his prescient book *Future Shock* in the 1970s.

As a result of this rapid transformation of knowledge, schools are going to have to become ever more equipped to somehow absorb rapidly transformed knowledge and information into their curricula, which means almost certainly that they are going to have to create new structures that will allow them to effectively do this. Yet it seems that the structure of the modern classroom has yet to undergo these transformative changes that will allow teachers and students to connect themselves to the rate of change that knowledge emanating from the world of adult expertise outside the classroom door is now undergoing.

Instead, it appears that classroom structures are for the most part still stuck, one way or another, in the same vertical, top-down model that has been around for about as long as any of us can remember, in which the teacher controls the flow of information and knowledge to his/her students; the result of this being that this model does not provide learning environments with the necessary amount of fluidity that students in their formative years are going to need if they are to effectively absorb the rate at which knowledge is now changing outside the classroom door.

At the same time, these older structures don't begin to address what appear to be the two new basic skills that have become necessary for success in our modern digital age—that is, the capacity for expanded, creative thinking within a specific area of expertise, and the ability to collaborate with others while turning that creativity into reality.

Therefore, this book is an attempt to address these two increasingly significant issues—the manner in which knowledge itself is now changing so rapidly, and the new skills necessary for success in our current information age—issues with which the modern classroom is going to have to deal if it is not going to soon become obsolete. That is, which structures for learning for young people in their formative years might parallel changes in the world of adult work that are taking place outside the schoolhouse door? And what are the new skills commensurate with those changes that students need to absorb if they are going to become successful in the world they are about to inherit?

However, it would seem that before we can effectively address either of these questions, we need to begin by addressing how our new digital world has changed both the manner in which either individuals or groups of people, particularly those who are members of the same profession, can immediately communicate with each other; and likewise, the manner in which knowledge and information itself now changes so quickly because of how rapidly it travels. Therefore, this is where we will begin.

Chapter One

A New Paradigm

During the 1980s, avant-garde English biochemist Rupert Sheldrake introduced the world to his concept of *morphic resonance*, which he argued was, and even purportedly provided evidence for, a theory that postulated that as certain species of animals acquire a new capacity (such as rats being taught new ways to negotiate a particular maze), the same species existing in different parts of the world immediately begins to acquire a similar capacity even though they are obviously separated geographically from the control group that first assimilated the new ability. In other words, a new piece of information had immediately traversed the supposed boundaries of time and space to become part of a particular species's behavior throughout different parts of the world.

Whether or not one is willing to admit that this type of somewhat spooky, otherworldly occurrence might actually exist, it seems entirely possible to suggest that Dr. Sheldrake's experiment could be used as a metaphor of sorts for how information and knowledge travel in our current information age and global marketplace. That is, they move so quickly that it almost seems at times that we are acquiring new facts and ideas about our world before we're even aware that we have done so. Hence, the lightning speed at which new information now travels, it would seem, is going to increasingly force all of us to reconsider what the optimal way is for us to assimilate it.

This is particularly true in terms of how we educate young people in their formative years in a world in which new facts, ideas, and knowledge that they have recently acquired may not only have been already amended before they have had time to assimilate them, but that those same changes are now immediately available to anyone with a working Internet connection. What this means, of course, is that it is now so much easier for today's students to be out of touch with what others in different parts of the world have already assimilated.

In other words, the specifics of what students need to acquire in order to be competent or knowledgeable in a specific field of inquiry often changes so rapidly, largely due to the fact that information and knowledge now travel so quickly, that by the time some new idea or fact finds its way from the research lab or workplace to the modern classroom for students in their formative years, it has already undergone significant changes.

Recently, scientists working at the large Hadron particle collider in Switzerland discovered the long sought Higgs boson particle, one that proves that there is in fact an energy field all around us that in fact creates the matter that makes up our world. Around the same time, genetic researchers in Europe, the United Kingdom, and the United States, working together, provided evidence that debunks the previously accepted theory that only about 2 percent of the human genome is made up of the protein-coding genes that lead toward the growth of cells and viable organs; the rest having been referred to as "junk DNA." Now, however, this new study shows that as much as 80 percent of our DNA actually has some biochemical function.

In reading about these developments, one has to wonder how rapidly the relevant discoveries concerning the relationship between matter and energy, and the viability of a much larger percentage of our DNA than we had previously imagined will find their way into the modern classroom as young people learn basic physics and human biology.

Of course previously, if students, particularly those younger than secondary school age, didn't acquire this sort of information as part of their science curriculum, it might not have made all that much difference as long as they learned the basics of what they were studying. Now, however, it seems, simply because this type of advanced knowledge appears so rapidly and travels so quickly, it becomes easy to imagine how students who don't assimilate it might grow increasingly out of touch with what other students their age in different parts of the world have not only apprehended, but have even used to move into the study of other related, complex subject areas.

Of course, it can also be argued that advanced subject areas such as these are ones that young students have plenty of time to learn as they grow toward adulthood. However, a couple of dynamics present here actually transcend whether or not young minds are learning about new discoveries and innovations that are taking place in the research lab, the contemporary university, the workplace, or even the arts.

One is that as students in different parts of the world acquire increasingly advanced knowledge at a younger age, it seems entirely possible to suggest that what was once considered to be knowledge that was essential for children to acquire is going to be transformed into something much larger and more fluid. The other changing dynamic is simply that in order to be successful in this interconnected world and digital age that they will inherit, one in which information and knowledge are becoming increasingly complex, young people are going to need to develop a new set of skills that will allow them to learn whatever might be necessary for them to acquire.

Computer coding was once thought to be the exclusive domain of people such as Bill Gates or Mark Zuckerberg, young geniuses who had a great facility to turn code into intriguing programs. Now, however, coding is becoming more and more a skill that anyone who wants to become involved in not just computer programming, but also any other number of different endeavors, is going to need to learn in order to not end up finding themselves significantly behind the curve, so to speak. For instance, as the market for electronic publishing continues to grow, and as more and more writers of books, or newspaper or magazine articles publish their work electronically in formats such as Amazon Kindle, they are going to need to become facile at writing code in order to upload their work properly.

Furthermore, since writing code is very much a function of learning algebra, which many learning theorists and educators claim can best be learned at an early age, basic algebra might well increasingly become a basic skill that needs to be made available to children at a much younger age than was previously thought necessary. In addition, because the ability to transfer code into real world applications, such as books or articles, is very much a skill that involves a certain type of relational thinking, this too might well become a new skill that young people will increasingly need to develop.

In other words, the rapidly changing nature of writing and publishing in the digital age is almost certainly going to eventually influence whether or not a seemingly unrelated skill such as basic algebra might need to be taught to children at a younger age than was previously thought necessary. This demonstrates how significant changes in a particular area of the contemporary workplace might have an increasingly rapid effect on subject matter in the modern classroom, even those changes that at first might not seem so relevant. As a consequence of this, curricula will have to become ever more fluid and changeable if they are to meet the needs of today's students.

Also, the manner in which different occupations are so easily becoming assimilated into one another in Thomas Friedman's flat world is going to mean that the particular skill sets that are part of subject matters that prepare students for success in the global marketplace are going to be subject to ever greater change. To this end, the Partnership for 21st Century Skills, a national organization that advocates twenty-first century readiness for every student, has come up with a list of core subjects and themes relevant to success in our present age—ones in which current subject matter such as math, science, or language arts might be included.

These core subjects include areas such as civic literacy, global awareness, financial literacy, health literacy, environmental literacy, and visual literacy—the latter having to do with assisting young learners in developing the necessary visual acuity that will allow them to optimally employ the various digital devices that will be keys to their future success. In other words, students would learn traditional subject matter within the context of much larger, interdisciplinary themes that would be inclusive of them.

What is intriguing about this idea is its notion that as areas of learning that prepare today's students for our current information age grow larger, they likewise become more practical. That is, their elasticity becomes the key to allowing students to absorb the advanced, more fluid, and changeable knowledge they will need to acquire in order to become successful in the modern world.

For example, global awareness literacy, which concerns the ability of students to learn from and work collaboratively with individuals from different cultures, would of course need to somehow include traditional subject matter such as regional histories, cultural studies, or basic economics and mathematics, but would do so in a way such that these different subject areas would necessarily grow more expansive as they interact with each other more seamlessly.

What seems so important to realize in all this is that because of the speed at which information not only travels today, but also because of the rate at which information continually changes, or quickly becomes absorbed into other discoveries, areas of learning in our schools are going to have to become both more expansive and more flexible. On the other hand, the narrow subject matter that one finds in many of our schools today, particularly that which originates solely to produce certain results on standardized tests, or in order to adhere to a national core curriculum, might in the long run actually make it more difficult for young students to absorb rapidly changing, complex information and knowledge simply because the subjects' parameters are too narrow to allow them to do so.

Narrowly conceived subject matter likewise tends to stifle both creativity and curiosity in young students to the point where their minds grow less pliable in absorbing new, complex information and ideas. The reason for this is that there is less opportunity for them to realize for themselves interesting connections and relationships that might exist in a large field of information and knowledge, and in so doing, absorb it more expansively. That is, if young people have a certain area of learning presented to them as broadly as possible so that there are a large number of connections to be made, and important relationships to be conceived within it, then there is a much greater chance that they will be able to absorb it even as it rapidly changes in the world outside school.

There were three twelve-year-old boys who learned theoretical physics with me at our school as an outgrowth of a conversation I had with them, when I mentioned that I was reading Stephen Hawking's *A Brief History of*

Time. During the conversation, I alluded to some of the nearly unbelievable things I had learned from the book that were actually well-established, scientific facts, such as the earth's movement around the sun being a result of the bending of the fabric of space by the sun's mass. After further discussing Hawking's book, we decided to work together to familiarize ourselves more fully with the field of theoretical physics.

Rather quickly, the learning between the four of us became entirely open-ended, egalitarian, and horizontal in nature simply because I did not have the sort of knowledge or expertise about the subject that would cause me to establish any type of preconceived, well-established boundaries while teaching it. I would bring in certain activities that I had gone home and designed in advance, such as the space-time diagrams for elementary particle collisions that the students could complete, diagrams that were similar to what professional physicists at well-known high-speed accelerators employ when they study the constituents of matter by colliding subatomic particles, and then the three students would set to work designing their own space-time diagrams.

As an outgrowth of working with activities such as these, one or more of the boys would usually grow interested in another aspect of the study of the physical universe, and I would then go home and design another activity that would meet that particular curiosity. Eventually, by following one interest to the next, we found our way—of course at a level that we could all comprehend—into such concerns as Einstein's theories of special and general relativity, Werner Heisenberg's uncertainty principle having to do with attempts to measure subatomic matter, and the endeavor by contemporary physicists to discover a unified field theory, which would unite as one the four known forces at work in the universe.

Most importantly, if some new, startling development had occurred in the world of physical science, such as the discovery of the Higgs boson particle, we would have been able to easily assimilate it into our own learning (provided we were able to comprehend it) simply because our subject matter of physical science had remained so broadly conceived. In addition, the way we shared information and knowledge with each other concerning the physical universe was much closer to the manner in which young people today are used to sharing information with each other in the world of social networking. That is, in the same non-hierarchical, egalitarian manner not based on the top-down authority of a particular expert.

Granted, this is an example of three extremely bright young people approaching subject matter that is probably more complex than what most young people, even secondary students, might learn during the course of their schooling. Yet the principle of allowing areas of learning to remain large, open-ended, and elastic in order that advanced knowledge from our rapidly changing information age can be assimilated into them remains exactly the same.

In addition to the speed at which information now travels in our digital age, and how it tends to so rapidly change, there is also the issue of how immediate, easy access to advanced knowledge, which everyone now enjoys, has so thoroughly changed the nature of our relationship to it. That is to say, as more and more people gain access to the same information and the same tools for obtaining that information—be they the latest iPhone, advancements in work-flow technology, or simply Google—the sources of knowledge and information will reside less and less in the hands of a few so-called experts, and will instead be made immediately available to everyone.

What this means is that knowledge is now residing not so much in the hands of a limited number of people who can disseminate it to others, but more in the hands of whoever can retrieve it. Of course, what this also means is that, as this dynamic of greatly increased information sharing becomes ever more a reality, success in our new digital age will become less a matter of obtaining knowledge and information that others do not possess, and more a function of how to creatively employ the same information to which everyone now has immediate access.

Hence, the primary purpose of educating students in their formative years, it would seem, is going to increasingly need to change from not just teaching them subject matter they are going to need to acquire in order to succeed as adults, but likewise assisting them in learning how to creatively use facts and ideas that are already readily available to others.

Cognitive theorists such as Jean Piaget have realized for a long time now that, if allowed to do so, children go about discovering their world in much the same manner as great scientists do. That is, children create their intelligence and the strength of their cognitive structures primarily through interactions with their world that are genuinely intriguing to them, and not nearly so much out of predetermined information, knowledge, and skills that have been handed to them in advance.

As noted cognitive theorist Howard Gardner puts it, each child must construct his own forms of knowledge painstakingly over time, with each tentative action or hypothesis representing whatever his current attempt to make sense of his world is until eventually he is able to internalize mental operations that formerly were carried out only in the world of concrete objects. This means that children optimally go about making sense of their world, and thus developing their intelligence, much as great scientists go about making their discoveries—by making sense of cause-effect relations in the sort of open-ended, creative manner that allows them free exploration.

So how do we educate young people to employ this same innate approach to their learning that they inherently possessed as young children, and that is often conditioned out of them by their subsequent schooling and upbringing, to learn creatively in a digital age that is going to increasingly demand it of them? This would seem to be the most relevant question as schooling in the twenty-first century moves forward.

As they stand now, most of our schools are designed to teach students predetermined curricula that educators believe will allow them to absorb highly specific information and skills at a level of competency that can then be tested by certain standardized measurements employed to evaluate whatever learning has taken place. This model, of course, is the genesis of such programs as No Child Left Behind, Race to the Top implemented by the Obama administration, or the proposed national core curriculum gaining increasing favor in a number of states.

However, if students in their formative years are to envision various subjects as creatively as they might in preparation for the world they are about to inherit, it seems they will first need to develop the capacity to relate different facts, skills, and information in new and different ways. That is, if students are going to be able to envision areas of knowledge expansively and to proceed with them in unique ways, they will need to increasingly develop the ability to relate seemingly disparate pieces of information, and even whole subjects, as part of an organic whole.

This is where social networking sites such as Facebook or Twitter, it would seem, might make a significant contribution. In the summer of 2011, an article appeared in *The New York Times* detailing how various school districts around the country had been attempting to block Facebook on school computers in order to prevent students from spending time on the site, only to have students outwit teachers and administrators by using proxy servers to get around the digital blockades imposed upon them. Unfortunately, in addition to getting drawn into a silly cat and mouse game with students whose computer skills no doubt far surpassed those who were attempting to block them, it seems that these same administrators had been blind to a real opportunity.

That is, they could have used the Facebook platform itself to turn social networks into learning networks that would connect those from the world of professional expertise with students of all different ages. For example, a twelve-year-old in one of these schools who was studying cell biology and how cancer spreads could potentially receive information from a medical researcher, doing significant genetic research, working at one of the large research hospitals somewhere in the world. Or a middle or high school civics class that was studying the United States Constitution by conducting mock trials could have asked relevant questions, and possibly received relevant answers, from a federal judge in Washington, D.C.

As a result of expanding subject areas more fully by connecting academic learning with the world of professional expertise vis-à-vis social networking sites like Facebook, the sort of relational thinking that is going to be increasingly important in our present digital age might be stimulated exponentially in young students simply because areas of learning, such as basic biology or civics, would now actually take place in the highly interconnected world of professional expertise that exists outside the schoolhouse door. Also, in an age in which most young people acquire new knowledge more through the endless information sharing that now takes place online, rather than by having it necessarily given to them by authorities and experts who exclusively possess that knowledge, the role of the classroom teacher is obviously going to have to change so that students are learning in the same horizontal, egalitarian manner that they have been doing for some time now in the digital world outside of school. In other words, when so many young people learn simply by Googling, the role of the traditional classroom teacher who stands in front of her class, imparting knowledge to them while they sit immobile, increasingly becomes woefully out of synch with the manner in which those students have been learning outside of school.

Cathy Davidson, professor of interdisciplinary studies at Duke University, and author of the 2011 book, *Now You See It: How the Brain Science of Attention Will Transform the Way We Live, Work, and Learn*, writes of how anyone born after 1985 came into a world organized by different principles of information gathering and knowledge searching than someone whose birthday preceded the Internet. Therefore, Davidson claims, the brains of those younger people are literally hardwired differently from ours. Whether or not this is true, and there is of course much evidence existing on either side of this debate, it is certainly the case that young people born after the advent of our digital age tend to have a much different relationship to information and knowledge than previous generations did.

People born after 1985 have grown up in a world in which it has become increasingly easier for them to seamlessly insert their own interests into the enormous, interconnected world that they can experience simply by turning on their computer. As a result, it appears to be more than a little obvious that when those same interests then run into the blockades of preconceived, test-driven subject matter taking place in their classrooms, there is bound to be reaction and aversion.

Of course, the matter would have to be studied thoroughly, and empirical data provided. Yet, it seems possible that at least one of the reasons for the increase in bullying of students by each other that now takes place in so many of our schools, and for the increasing dropout rates, might be the confluence of our current, high-stakes testing culture with the digital age in which today's young people were born. That is, many of today's students may be reacting to how they are being taught in results-driven environments compared to what they regularly experience when they are not in school, plugged into their computer or iPhone. Hence, they begin to pick on other students as a means of releasing their frustration—or else simply drop out of school altogether.

At the same time, simply making all the new technologies that are part of our rapidly expanding digital age readily available to students is not necessarily going to solve the growing disconnect between classroom environments and the world that young people experience outside the schoolhouse door. Rather, it would seem, what is needed is a fundamental change in the actual structure of the modern classroom so that it can allow students to learn in a manner that is commensurate with how they are absorbing new facts and ideas when they are not in school.

In fact, simply bringing in new technologies won't make much difference if the actual structures of learning milieus aren't first changed in order that these new technologies can be properly incorporated into them. Khan Academy has been getting quite a bit of attention from both education writers and the mainstream press in general, with a segment about it appearing in the fall of 2011 on CBS's *Sixty Minutes*. Created by Bengali American educator Sal Khan, the nonprofit educational organization provides free online videos, via YouTube, for students in their formative years in all different subjects.

Khan has been praised by a number of educators, and by Bill Gates himself, who believes that the videos allow students to learn more efficiently because they are able to do so individually with a comfort level that works for them, and because they allow classroom teachers to provide their students with more individual attention. In fact, a growing number of teachers are using the Khan videos in their classrooms by assigning them as homework, and then giving students the necessary attention the following day that will allow them to properly digest what they had apprehended the previous evening. Many teachers claim that bringing Khan into their classroom has indeed allowed them to give their students the sort of individual attention that they had not been able to previously provide.

Yet, at the same time, there appears to be a certain concern that needs to be addressed. This is simply that, if the students in these classrooms are still learning as they sit immobile at their computers, in the same hierarchical, top-down manner that takes place in most classrooms today—with the teacher controlling and filtering the flow of information and knowledge to her students, this time vis-à-vis the videos—then is more creative learning actually being implemented?

In other words, it seems hard to imagine how a classroom that employs Khan Academy is necessarily changing its basic structure in a manner that will allow its students to effectively process and absorb rapidly changing information and knowledge from the world outside the schoolhouse door if the potentially open-ended collaborative nature of learning in that classroom is still not part of its basic structure. Therefore, the fundamental question, rather than asking what new, twenty-first century technologies can we bring into our classrooms, would appear to be this: How can we change the actual structure of our classrooms in a manner that not only makes them more receptive to the ever-changing, rapid transfer of knowledge in our current information age, but also permits the entrance of new technologies in a manner in which these new digital devices don't simply serve to strengthen outdated, unnecessarily restrictive milieus?

One possible answer might be found in the growth of project-based learning, something that is increasingly being implemented in ways that have been highly successful in schools. These projects involve students' collaborating as a group in order to solve real-world problems, using the relevant technologies found in the world of professional expertise, and in so doing, learning how to weave together the particulars of specific subject matter that has formerly been taught to them in isolation.

Hence, because their learning is collaborative—and always active—in ways similar to how problems are being increasingly solved in our digital age, the situation of a lone teacher controlling the behavior of an entire class of students while they sit immobile and she directs the flow of information and knowledge seldom rears its ugly head. In addition, the open-ended nature of the projects themselves often permits students to approach subject matter much more creatively than they might have been previously able to do.

Examples of such project-based learning have in the past included

- a high school geometry class at Mountlake Terrace High School in Washington designing a state of the art school for the year 2050, a project that involved creating a site plan, making architectural drawings of rooms, drawing up a budget, and writing a narrative report;
- second graders at Newsome Park Elementary School in Newport News, Virginia, who were curious about the cystic fibrosis from which one of their classmates suffered inviting experts to talk to them about the disease, then writing up their research using graphs and PowerPoint; and
- a project at the Mott Hall School in New York's Harlem district in which a group of fifth graders, working together, designed their own kites on the computer by using the concepts of ratio and proportion—and then made the kites by hand.

Again, what is significant about project-based learning, even more than their potential use of new digital technologies, is that it gives students the opportunity to share information and collaborate in ways identical to how this is done in the information age outside the schoolhouse door. That is, young people are learning how to employ the very model for success that they will need to absorb as they move toward adulthood.

In addition, project-based learning gives them the capacity to rapidly absorb new facts and ideas into what they have previously learned simply because areas of learning with which they are becoming acquainted have remained fluid and elastic. For example, the students in Harlem who were designing kites on their computers would have been able, by working collaboratively and using the sort of open-ended curriculum that they were employing, to incorporate many more useable facts from the worlds of both mathematics and physical science than if these were being taught to them by a single classroom teacher using a predetermined curriculum.

IDEAS FOR REFLECTION

The foundations for a new paradigm that permits teachers and students to share information with each other in the same collaborative manner that is now increasingly becoming the staple of the new digital age in which we are living, and that will allow them to more easily absorb rapidly changing knowledge into what they are already learning, is most likely not going to occur unless certain significant structural changes in the modern classroom happen first. This means clearing away all those things that stand in the way of more open-ended learning transpiring. Among these might be predetermined curricula that are rigidly in place prior to students' entering school at the beginning of the school year in order to insure that the students achieve certain scores on high-stakes standardized tests. Because the subject matter employed is too narrowly defined, another obstacle might be highly specific areas of learning that make it extremely difficult, if not impossible, for young people to apprehend all the significant relationships that might exist within those areas. And, seemingly as much as anything, a hierarchical, top-down model of teaching and learning in which a single teacher essentially controls the flow of information and knowledge to the students in her classroom may stand in the way of more open-ended learning.

There is also something else. This is the question of whether or not one can implement approaches to educating young people in their formative years that are essentially based on empirical data, such as standardized test scores, which then become validations of successful learning, while one is likewise attempting to facilitate open-ended, collaborative learning environments that stress creative thinking. That is, can the two dynamics ever exist simultaneously?

For if it is the case that our current results-driven approach to learning, emanating from our national testing program, the Obama administration's Race to the Top, or the recently proposed national core standards do indeed narrow subject matter and stifle creativity, then we may well be actually lessening the chances that our young people have to be successful as they enter the present digital age with its prevalent collaborative information sharing and rapid transfer of knowledge.

Therefore, it seems necessary that we begin to examine the structure of the modern classroom with this particular question in mind. That is, are today's classrooms remnants from a different age that is no longer relevant? For if this is indeed the case, then it would seem that solving our current education crisis might not be so much a matter of bringing better teachers into our schools, or adopting more useful standards or a core curriculum, as of fundamentally changing the structure of classrooms themselves.

Furthermore, if educators believe that creative learning can be engendered in young students, particularly those in elementary and middle schools, simply because classroom teachers introduce innovative lesson plans or bring in new digital devices, but then do little to fundamentally change the basic nature of their classroom milieus, then certain structural barriers will inevitably begin to stand in the way, the same ones that have stood in the way now for decades.

Consequently, the following chapters in this work attempt to suggest exactly what sort of significant structural changes need to be implemented if today's students are going to learn in the sort of innovative way that will prepare them for the world they are about to inherit. For it seems obvious that as the nature of relations in the worlds of commerce, industry, technology, and the arts becomes increasingly horizontal and egalitarian, rather than remaining essentially vertical and in the hands of a limited number of experts, models for how young people might learn in this new digital age are consequently going to have to change dramatically. Otherwise the latter has little chance of being in synch with the former.

Chapter Two

Barriers to Success

Mihaly Csikszentmihalyi is a well-known Hungarian psychologist who in his seminal work, *Flow: The Psychology of Optimal Experience,* outlined his theory that people are most happy and productive when they are in a state of what he calls *flow*—a state of concentration or complete absorption with the activity or situation at hand. That is, the person is completely immersed in what he or she is doing. Csikszentmihalyi went on to say that in order to achieve a flow state, a balance must be struck between the challenge of the task and the skill of the performer. If the task is too easy or too difficult, flow cannot occur. In addition, both skill level and challenge level must be matched and high; and even if skill level and challenge level are low and matched, then apathy results.

A perfect example of the positive attributes of a "flow state" occurred one day at our school in Evanston during a lesson in which several children between the ages of eight and eleven began filling out a long piece of mural paper that we had rolled out on the floor on which they were drawing different parts of the electromagnetic spectrum (i.e., visible light waves, radio waves, x-rays, etc.). As they did so, one of the students, a ten-year-old boy, began to make the connection for himself between how stretched out the waves were as he drew them, how powerful they were, and which ones were potentially dangerous. In other words, he had suddenly entered a world that he had not only discovered for himself, but one that was highly unpredictable, and in which his skill and challenge levels matched each other perfectly.

In those moments, it was obvious how his inner world was being immediately energized. His impressions were stronger, his curiosity exponentially piqued, and his initiative obviously emboldened as he picked up one marker pen after another and attempted to draw what seemed to him to be a close approximation of infrared or cosmic rays. At the same time, because he was entirely focused on this new, fascinating world that he had unexpectedly entered, he was completely grounded in what he was assimilating. Finally, certain difficulties in concentrating, and a significant amount of reactive anger that had been generated within him as a result of this, both of which had been seen by not only teachers at our school, but also by adults at other schools he had attended, now vanished as he focused intently on the unrolled paper directly in front of him.

In 1988, Jeanne Nakamura, now professor in the School of Behavioral and Organizational Sciences at Claremont Graduate University, conducted a study at a Chicago high school for the sciences, one in which all the students had tested similarly high in math proficiency, but who were ranked by their teachers as being either high or low achievers. During the course of her study, Nakamura used Csikszentmihalyi's ideas concerning a flow state to analyze the moods of students learning math.

What she found in her study was that the high achievers reported that studying gave them the sort of pleasing, absorbing challenge of the flow state 40 percent of the time, while for the low achievers, this flow state occurred only 16 percent of the time. In fact, more often than not, for these lesser achievers, academic learning resulted only in anxiety.

It would seem to be fairly obvious that this flow state the successful students in Nakamura's study had entered, and that the young student at our school had suddenly entered might indeed be a key to assisting young people to learn in a manner that best prepares them for the sort of fluid, rapidly changing world outside the schoolhouse door that they will soon encounter, a world that will increasingly demand highly creative approaches to various fields of endeavor. This is true, as much as anything, because of the integral relationship that might exist between the flow state and the creative mind itself.

As Csikszentmihalyi puts it, creative thinkers tend to be those who exist in a state of flow. That is, they are completely absorbed in whatever task they are engaged, and in addition, their skill level and the challenge of their task are not only perfectly matched, but likewise exist at a certain high level—this being true for young people learning mathematics, science, or reading as much as for great artists or scientists. Therefore, with this is mind, the question relative to engendering creative learning in young people as they prepare to enter our challenging information age would seem to be this: Which classroom structures might stimulate a state of flow and creative absorption in students and which might effectively kill these things?

The basic structure of most classrooms today is well-known to anyone who has ever attended school. Students sit immobile at their desks while the classroom teacher walking among them controls the flow of information and knowledge to which they are expected to adhere through highly preconceived subject matter. Eventually, the students are tested and graded on what they are expected to learn, and the results of these standardized tests, as well as the grades the students are given, become a definition of how well the student is learning whatever he or she is expected to absorb.

Even in most progressive schools in which students are given more freedom of movement and a certain hand in negotiating their curriculum, or in which letter grades are not given, the basic dynamic tends to be pretty much the same. That is, the information and knowledge that the students are expected to absorb flows in a vertical fashion from the teacher to the students, with students then being asked to demonstrate, vis-à-vis their performance on standardized tests or by adhering to performance standards implemented by their teachers, that they have indeed acquired whatever others have decided they need to assimilate by a certain point in time.

In addition, curricula are becoming ever more standardized in order to be certain that material that appears on standardized tests becomes a significant part of classroom learning. Certain scores are being increasingly necessary if schools are to continue to receive funding, classroom teachers are to be judged to be successful, or parents are to keep their children enrolled in various private or charter schools.

Yet, despite the hue and cry that is going on these days among educators who decry the pervasive use of these tests and how they are in fact producing standardized learning and narrowed curricula (which is indeed true), still it may be the case that, as damaging as our testing culture might be, the greater problem relative to properly preparing today's students for the current digital age, could have more to do with the improper relationship that now exists between the structure found in most contemporary classrooms—even more progressive ones—and the inner lives of students who are attempting to learn in them. This is where Csikszentmihalyi's idea of a flow state relative to creative thinking and learning might have much to offer us, the question being this: What type of classroom structure will facilitate the sort of complete absorption by young students in whatever they are learning, that in which this absorption takes place because students' skill and challenge levels are perfectly matched? For it seems fairly obvious that if young people are going to learn to relate information and knowledge creatively while they learn, they must first be absorbed in and properly challenged by the subject matter they are attempting to apprehend. Otherwise, they will tend to miss most of the significant relationships and connections to which they might have access.

In 2007, the New Commission on the Skills of the American Workforce, a high-powered, bipartisan assembly of education, government, and business leaders, met and released a blueprint for rethinking American education from pre-kindergarten to grade twelve and beyond—a blueprint that the commission was convinced would better prepare students for the current global economy.

In the report they released, *Tough Choices or Tough Times*, they recommended that several new capacities will be important for students to develop in preparation for eventually entering the current information age and global marketplace. Among these were the capacity to see patterns where others see only chaos, the ability to think across academic disciplines, and the capacity to distinguish between information that can be usefully employed and that which cannot. In other words, their report focused heavily on how educators might assist students in making innovative and creative thinking a significant part of their academic learning.

Citing that the new factors in our global economy that will lead toward continued economic success by different countries are creativity and innovation, the commission also stated that creative, innovative thinking in a particular area of endeavor is not only a matter of knowledge and expertise in that area. It also depends, now more than ever, on being able to combine disparate elements in a number of seemingly different areas. In addition, the report reiterated, this will only happen in circumstances in which a creative person is allowed to fail many times in order to eventually succeed; and that those who are most successful respond poorly to extrinsic motivation.

In taking the findings of the commission concerning creative thinking and innovation, as well as the thoughts of Mihaly Csikszentmihalyi on creativity vis-à-vis a flow state, and then transporting these to how classrooms might engender more creative thinking and learning, one particular question comes immediately to mind. In what ways might both the structure of contemporary classrooms and schools, as well as the nature of how subject matter is being taught to young learners be standing in the way of the type of learning in which today's young people need to be engaged in order to be prepared for the world they will eventually inherit?

One dynamic that certainly needs to be considered is the lack of opportunity that students might have to move freely within their learning environment. That is, in many classrooms today, young people are confined to a desk or table much of the time while they learn. Hence, those students lose the opportunity to direct their own learning; this being so even if their teacher has negotiated learning plans with them in which they have been encouraged to either pursue what interests them in relation to a particular subject matter, or to develop their own standards of accountability for which they are willing to hold themselves responsible.

Particularly with kindergarten through eight grade students, without freedom of movement throughout the day within their particular learning environment, there can be no true initiative simply because the two tend to be bound together within young people as part of the same forward movement toward whatever is engaging them. That is to say, it is simply not possible for young people to come fully into contact with what is leaving the strongest impression upon them, or truly piquing their curiosities, unless they are allowed to consistently move physically toward it. Hence, they likewise often lose the opportunity to view various areas of learning as expansively as they otherwise might and, in so doing, lose the opportunity to discover that place of creative absorption where their skill and challenge levels match each other perfectly.

Even more important, relative to young people's learning in a manner that will best prepare them for success in the current information age, is the fact that in those classrooms in which students are constrained for a significant period of time each day to a certain space in the room—in most cases a desk—and in which they are allowed to move freely around their classroom only with the permission of their teacher, many important aspects of their particular learning environment become immediately inaccessible to them. These aspects have to do largely with the activities and subject matters to which other students are attending.

On the other hand, when students are allowed to move freely around their classroom, all of the possibilities inherent in their particular learning milieu become immediately and seamlessly accessible to them because they are allowed to move freely toward them. Hence, it becomes exponentially easier for them to make important connections within a specific area of learning that they are considering, or with other areas related to it, and in so doing discover for themselves Csikszentmihalyi's place of creative absorption, than it would be if they were sitting immobile at their desks, as they are in many of today's classrooms.

Yet, whenever this sort of immobility is present, students often not only lose the opportunity to consistently engage in the sort of creative thinking that is going to become so important to them in the world they are about to inherit, but just as significantly, they lose the opportunity to collaborate with one another in examining a particular area of learning, which they would possess if they were allowed to move freely during the course of their school day. Hence, over time, they are not able to experience, as they otherwise might, the type of collaboration with others in solving problems that has now become so important for success in our current digital age.

In addition to how the lack of free movement that is present in many of today's classrooms diminishes the opportunity for more creative, collaborative learning by students, there is also the matter of how the increasingly rigid standards that are now seeping into the educational landscape might be doing the very same thing. The recent Common Core Standards Initiative, sponsored by the National Governors Association and the Council of Chief State School Officers, and now adopted by forty-five states, was originally announced on June 1, 2009. Its stated purpose is to "provide a consistent, clear understanding of what students are expected to learn so that teachers and parents know what they need to do to help them." In addition, the report goes on to state, "standards are designed to be robust and relevant to the real world, reflecting the knowledge and skills that our young people need for success in college and careers."

In other words, the standards, which are a direct result of the accountability movement that swept education in the late 1980s and early 1990s in conjunction with E. D. Hirsch, Jr.'s core knowledge curriculum and foundation, which detailed the exact skills and knowledge that students at each grade level should be expected to acquire through such books as *What Your Fifth Grader Needs to Know*, attempt to establish the core skills and knowledge that are deemed necessary for all students to acquire regardless of the dynamics of their local communities.

Standards for mathematics and English language arts were released on June 2, 2010, with a majority of the states adopting the standards in subsequent months. The math standards for kindergarten through fifth grade students include such general areas as basic operations and algebraic thinking; number and operations in base 10; measurement and data; and geometry. For grades six through eight they include the number system, expressions and equations, geometry, and statistics and probability. The writing standards, which begin at grade six, include such things for students in grade six through eight as the ability to use precise language and domain-specific vocabulary to inform about or explain a topic, establish and maintain a formal style and objective tone, and provide a concluding statement or section that follows from and supports the information or explanation presented.

Of course, there is nothing wrong with both teachers and students having a general idea of what knowledge and skills are important for young people to acquire as they reach a certain age. Yet, relative to engendering creative thinking and learning in students in preparation for their future success in our current digital age, it would seem that the problem comes when such standards begin to actually direct learning paths inside classrooms, rather than simply providing indications of what basic skills and knowledge young people need to acquire.

Several major problems with the standards relative to the new age we have entered were elucidated by veteran teacher, curriculum designer, and author Marion Brady in a blog post that Valerie Strauss published as her column in *The Washington Post* on August 21, 2012. Among them was Brady's contention that core standards do a couple of damaging things relative to preparing students for the age of fluid, changing information and knowledge that they are about to enter. One is that by introducing static subject matter to students in an ever-changing world, we are preparing them for what Brady terms a "Titanic-deck-chair" exercise. What this means is that in an ever-changing, dynamic world of professional expertise, certain core standards that may have originally prepared students for what they would need to know can easily become rapidly outdated to the point where they actually become barriers to students' apprehending other, more advanced subject matter that might become more relevant.

For example, as success in any number of different areas of the contemporary workplace, such as computer technology, become increasingly a function of how well one is able to employ algebraic thought to write computer code, one can easily see how any type of rigid standards applied to learning mathematics and algebra can easily become immediate barriers to students' future success simply because they inevitably block the study of more relevant areas of algebraic thought and operations.

In addition, as the necessity for learning certain skills filters down from the dynamics of the contemporary workplace, what were once thought to be skills that were too advanced for students to learn at a certain age are inevitably going to be introduced into various schools and learning environments around the world. Hence, core standards that become rapidly outdated are going to inevitably stand in the way of students' learning more advanced skills and knowledge that have suddenly become both necessary and significant elsewhere.

This seems particularly true in terms of science curricula in that new discoveries and inventions that are immediately available to everyone on the planet make it inevitable that what was once considered to be core knowledge in a particular area of science might be rapidly no longer relevant. In this regard, one thinks immediately of how the recent discovery of the Higgs boson particle immediately changes what students need to know, even at a rather young age, if they are to be properly educated about the relationship between matter and energy. This would appear to be particularly significant when many schools today still teach Isaac Newton's theory of gravitation, which was replaced nearly one hundred years ago by Einstein's Theory of General Relativity, as the final word on the subject.

Brady also makes mention of the idea that common core standards inevitably kill innovative thinking. This, of course, seems rather obvious when one considers how rigidly preconceived curricula, whether they emanate directly from national standards or simply from the curriculum of a local school, can so easily constrict subject matter. This is so simply because when students are required to adhere to various subject areas vis-à-vis highly predetermined curricula, they lose the opportunity to consider them more expansively.

That is, young people have less opportunity to realize for themselves interesting connections and relationships that might exist in a larger field of information and knowledge, and in so doing, to think more creatively. Yet if students have a certain area of learning presented to them as expansively as possible so that there are a large number of connections to be made and important relationships to be conceived within it, then there is a much greater chance that they will be able to develop the initiative to apprehend the subject area in unique ways.

On the other hand, if early in their lives, students are encouraged to focus on the specifics of predetermined areas of learning, rather than on how those specifics might be part of integrated wholes, they will most likely end up leading themselves directly away from approaching facts, information, and subject matter uniquely and originally. Then, as their minds become increasingly comfortable traversing the sort of well-worn grooves into which they have become accustomed while absorbing these specifics in order to please adults, this will increasingly tend to become an entrenched reality within them as they approach adulthood.

Howard Gardner, in his book *The Unschooled Mind: How Children Think and How Schools Should Teach*, mentions how the mind of a five-year-old contains a swirl of symbols, theories, and concepts that remain to be sorted out in a more secure manner. Therefore, much of this effort in the ensuing years has very much to do with calming or harnessing this raw mind. Yet, Gardner adds, as much as this regularization can have a positive effect, the process can also easily limit a child's imagination or reinforce biases and stereotypes that at this point have not yet become thoroughly entrenched.

Therefore, it would seem that before one introduces highly specific, preconceived curricula that emanate from such programs as the Common Core Standards Initiative, one should first carefully consider the possible effects on young peoples' cognitive lives as they move into the highly malleable periods of what Piaget refers to as symbolic thought and concrete operations, during which their mental acuity begins to solidify. This would appear to be particularly true as young people prepare for adult life in a digital age in which knowledge and information not only are available to all so quickly, but also change so rapidly. That is, if the minds of young people become conditioned through rigidly preconceived subject matter to operate in well-worn grooves, they will inevitably become less adaptable to the rate of rapid change as they approach adulthood.

Likewise, educators should be wary of the effect that our current obsession with evaluating learning through the use of standardized test scores has on the development of the creative thinking that young people will need for success in our current age. Particularly relevant, of course, is how subject matter becomes inevitably narrowed in order that students achieve certain test scores, with items that are to be tested actually becoming the curriculum itself in many cases.

As more and more educators have become aware of this dynamic, the opposition to our national testing program has grown extreme, with some teachers now actually refusing to test their students in the face of pressure from school boards, administrators, and principals to do so. Most of this resistance tends to stem from anger over how standardized tests narrow subject matter to the point where it can't be expanded to its full potential so that teachers and students can apprehend it as creatively as they might. Opposition also stems from the point of view that successful teaching and learning often can't be measured empirically. Hence a standardized test is an inaccurate measure of how well teachers are teaching and students are learning.

Yet beyond these two factors, as significant as they might be, there would appear to be a particular dynamic mentioned in the report by the New Commission on the Skills of the American Workforce which might be even more significant in terms of how students might retain the necessary malleability of mind to which Howard Gardner alludes relative to their eventual entrance into a global marketplace in which perceiving significant relationships and collaborating with others have become such important skills. This is the commission's concern that often when students are evaluated by standardized testing, they are asked to come up with one right answer in response to various questions. Hence, they tend to be actually penalized for coming up with the occasional, creative, outside-the-box thinking in regard to various subject matter.

In March of 2011, there was an article in the *Chicago Sun-Times* that reported that Chicago Public School eighth graders racked up the fourth worst science scores among seventeen big city districts on a national science test, with the article proceeding to decry the fact that the city's African American eighth graders tied their Baltimore counterparts in producing the worst African American science scores among the nation's large urban school districts.

The article included a sample question from the test the students were given, which was, "Why do mountain climbers at high elevations use oxygen tanks to help them breathe?" The list of possible multiple-choice answers included: the ozone layer drawing oxygen out of the earth's atmosphere; the density of the earth's atmosphere at higher elevations; or how radiation from the sun at higher elevations might split oxygen molecules into their component atoms, thus making the air unbreathable.

Although it was reported that only 59 percent of the Chicago students taking the test gave what was deemed to be the correct answer, which is that the atmosphere is less dense at higher elevations, there may indeed be something far more troubling than this inability of young people to answer this one question when viewed in terms of the sort of creative thought that will be necessary for young people to develop as they approach the information age as adults—particularly in regard to their possible entry into the world of science. That is, constricting the range of possible answers within such narrow parameters makes it more difficult for any young person taking the test to think as creatively as they might otherwise be allowed to do. For example, some mountain climbers are in fact able to climb high peaks such as Mt. Everest without the use of bottled oxygen. Hence, the reason why other climbers use it might have to more with human physiology than it does with thin air. In addition, the second potential answer, that the sun's radiation splits oxygen molecules into atoms, may be true in our own atmosphere, but not in other parts of the universe. Therefore, one can easily see how excluding this possibility from consideration might effectively kill the sort of expansive, creative thinking that might otherwise take place in relation to the original question.

Increasingly, schools and classroom teachers, under the gun to produce higher test scores, are developing curricula directly from questions that they know their students will be asked on standardized tests. That is, teaching is often being redefined as test preparation. Seventy-nine percent of teachers surveyed by *Education Week* said they spent "a great deal" or "somewhat" of their time instructing students in test-taking skills, and 53 percent said they used state practice tests a great deal or somewhat.

As a result of this, it is easy to see how expansive, outside-the-box, creative thinking might be directly affected when test questions that are too narrowly defined become the curriculum itself. Kyung Hee Kim, professor of education at the College of William and Mary, analyzed scores on a battery of measures of creativity—called the Torrance Tests of Creative Thinking (TTCT)—collected from normative samples of schoolchildren in kindergarten through twelfth grade over several decades. According to Kim's analyses, the scores on these tests at all grade levels began to decline somewhere between 1984 and 1990 and have continued to decline ever since. In some cases, the drops in scores were highly significant statistically and in some cases were very large.

Furthermore, according to Kim's research, although all aspects of young people's creativity have declined, the biggest decline he found was in the measure called Creative Elaboration, which assesses a student's ability to take a particular idea and expand on it in an interesting and novel way. In this measure of the age group between kindergarten and twelfth grade, Kim found that scores fell by more than one standard deviation, meaning that 85 percent of children in 2008 scored lower on this measure than did the average child in 1984.

When one considers that the Elementary and Secondary Education Act, which required standardized testing in public schools, was enacted in 1965, and that the more recent No Child Left Behind Act, which tied public school funding to standardized test scores, was passed in 2001, it would seem rather easy to believe that there may in fact be a direct statistical correlation between how often students have been tested during the past fifty years in our society and a potential decrease in their capacity to think creatively. It is now commonly believed by many that standards-based education and empirical testing of student abilities, as imperfect as they may be, are important keys to educating students in this country in a manner that will allow to compete with others from around the world as they approach adulthood. Yet is it possible that these two things, along with the fact that students in most classrooms today sit immobile much of the time while they learn, might actually be standing in the way of young people's being ultimately successful in our current digital age?

Indeed, it seems entirely possible that in a world in which not only information and knowledge flow so rapidly and change so quickly, but also in which entire professions undergo similar rapid changes, creative thinking will soon trump even the assimilation of knowledge as the most dominant key to future success—particularly when knowledge concerning almost any area of expertise is no further away than Google or any other information based website. If this is indeed the case, then just as our schools had to undergo significant changes during the early twentieth century in order to prepare students for the new industrial age that they would be entering, our schools seemingly need to undergo a similar transformation in preparing students for the current information and global marketplace.

Whereas before, the increasing division of labor that was part of the industrial age led to the need for schools to educate their students to ultimately assume increasingly specialized roles, now both the speed by which information is available to everyone, and the sort of tools that one can employ to access that information means that our schools likewise need to undergo significant changes. Only this time, the changes are in regard to preparing students for how to creatively use whatever information and knowledge they access. And although becoming proficient in how to effectively use the Internet, the latest digital technology, or the software inside one's computer to access and use connections and information as effectively as possible is of course significant, what seems even more important, particularly now that everyone around the world is rapidly gaining those same abilities, is learning how to approach knowledge, information, and new situations creatively and adaptively. For this is the sort of learning that will allow today's students, as they become adults, to in fact use that same creative thinking in confronting increasingly changing and complex, cutting-edge, workplace situations.

In addition, learning how to collaborate with others in achieving a common goal will likewise become an increasingly important capacity that young people will need to develop in terms of their future success. When Tom Friedman wrote *The World is Flat* in 2005, he spoke with former Hewlett Packard CEO Carly Fiorina, who told him that we had gone from a vertical chain of command for value creation to a much more horizontal one, meaning that innovation in companies like HP is coming more and more from horizontal collaboration among different departments and teams spread all over the globe.

As an example of this, she mentioned how HP, Cisco, and Nokia had collaborated on the development of a camera/cell phone that beams its digital

pictures to an HP printer that quickly prints them out. In other words, each company had developed a very sophisticated technological specialty, but that each was able to come up with something new only when its specialty was combined with the specialty of the other two companies.

When one considers that this sort of horizontal collaboration was occurring in the global marketplace before the emergence of Facebook, Twitter, the recent iPhones, or iPads that provide mobile access to the Internet at any time, or the recent popularity of online gaming strategies as a means of solving problems, it becomes even more obvious why horizontal collaboration in the global marketplace, among either companies or among individuals, has now gone from being something new and innovative to being, not only something vital and necessary, but also something that is now commonplace.

In fact, horizontal collaboration among businesses that run similar operations and produce similar products increasingly occurs; particularly as businesses realize that such collaboration can have a significant financial effect on operating costs without affecting the quality of their product. Recently, the U.S. Center for Automotive Research estimated that such collaboration could help different automobile manufacturers make production 40 percent more effective by sharing vehicle tooling platforms. Hence, creative collaboration among even companies that compete with each other for customers is becoming increasingly the norm.

And yet it seems that by requiring students in many of today's classrooms to assimilate preconceived curricula that are increasingly determined by both nationwide core standards and the need by schools, teachers, and administrators to produce certain scores on standardized tests or face consequences for not doing so, we may indeed be making it more difficult for young students to develop the capacity to approach subject matter and learning situations creatively, and to collaborate with others while doing so. In other words, the very two things that many educators believe will better prepare students for the new information age they are about to enter—assimilating predetermined core knowledge and skills, and demonstrating this assimilation by scoring well on standardized tests—may in fact be significant structural barriers, along with the immobility in their classrooms to which many of today's students are subjected as a result of these, which will ultimately prevent them from becoming more successful in the world they are about to inherit.

IDEAS FOR REFLECTION

The two most pressing questions related to preparing today's students for this new information age that they will soon enter would seem to be these: What new skills are needed for success in a world of increased information sharing and creative collaboration? And what classroom structures will best implement these skills? Yet it would seem that before we can answer either of these questions we need to begin to clear away remnants from an earlier industrial age that still exist in many of our classrooms—that in which standardized, overly specialized curricula were put in place to prepare students for the increasing division of labor that took place in the world at the beginning of the twentieth century.

For now that outside-the-box, creative thinking and horizontal collaboration have become the necessary ingredients for success in our new digital age, these would seem to be the qualities that we most need to facilitate in young learners. Yet it is hard to see how that can occur as long as standardized curricula, a results-driven approach to learning, and the immobility of students that exists in most classrooms today remain the norm. In fact, we may have actually reached the point, without realizing that we are doing so, in which we are actually educating young people in a way that will ultimately make it more difficult for them to succeed when they eventually enter the current information age and global marketplace.

Chapter Three

New Skills for a New Time

In *The World Is Flat*, Tom Friedman alludes to the fact that because occupations and businesses are becoming so rapidly absorbed into each other, lifetime employment at any business or company no longer exists, with adaptability of workers becoming increasingly a key to their future success. As a consequence of this, it would seem to be extremely important that contemporary workers develop a set of skills that allows them to think creatively no matter what their chosen profession or occupation is, rather than just developing a particular set of skills, in isolation from other skills, which allows them to be successful in one specific area of employment.

Obviously, this capacity to think creatively, if it is to flourish to the fullest degree possible, needs to begin in a person's life long before they apply for their first job. In fact, it needs to begin while that person is being educated during his formative years, when his or her cognition is still malleable in the manner in which learning theorists such as Howard Gardner or Jean Piaget say that it is.

More to the point, what skills will today's students need to develop in order to approach subject matter more creatively in preparation for their eventual entry into a global marketplace in which outside-the-box apprehension and adaptive thinking are becoming increasingly necessary in response to entire occupations and businesses becoming rapidly absorbed into one another?

Previously, developing the skills and knowledge necessary to perform a specific role in society was enough for a person to become successful. However, now that there is such fluidity in regard to not only occupations and businesses, but also in regard to the rapidly changing nature of the highly specific knowledge that is part of the modern workplace, it is extremely possible that the different ways in which one might relate and connect

31

knowledge and information creatively will become the new, primary basic skill that needs to be facilitated in young learners—rivaling even certain knowledge based skills and abilities that have stood for decades.

First, however, it would seem that if young learners are to effectively learn this new skill, they are going to need to acquire a corresponding set of other skills that will allow them to do so. These would be such things as: the ability to distinguish between knowledge and information that exists in isolation and that which can be related to other information and knowledge; the ability to identify different relationships that might be occurring between seemingly disparate pieces of information; the ability to connect different subject areas; the capacity to generalize specific types of relationships shared by different information within different subject areas; and the ability to distinguish between knowledge that must be learned and that which can simply be retrieved on the World Wide Web. For these are the skills that will enhance relational, creative investigation of a particular area of learning simply because they will make it easier for students to look for patterns and perceive connections whenever they are introduced to information and knowledge that may be new to them. In addition, these are highly specific skills that are going to need to be taught to young learners, just as the basic skills that young people need to acquire to learn to read, write, and work with numbers are presently taught to them.

For just as the ability to decode and blend different phonemes allows a child to learn to read more easily, so the ability to connect knowledge from different subject areas gives the student a broader field of information to choose from in developing his or her own creative learning progressions. Or just as an understanding of proper sentence structure permits a student to learn the skill of writing, so the ability to distinguish between knowledge that needs to be learned and that which can simply be retrieved makes one a more effective learner. Or just as an understanding of numerical hierarchies permits a child to add and subtract, so the ability to distinguish between knowledge and information that exists in isolation, and that which can be related, makes one a more creative learner.

In her 2010 paper, *Analogy and Classroom Mathematics Learning*, Lindsey Richland, Professor of Education at the University of California, Irvine, writes of how mathematical proficiency is directly related to a learner's ability to draw inferences from prior knowledge and instruction to solve previously unseen problems. To this end, she discusses a procedural fluency strand, that in which young learners are able to identify structural similarities between new problems and problems that they either previously solved or were instructed in how to solve.

This ability to identify actual structural similarities between new areas of learning and previous ones with which the learner is already familiar is exactly one of those new skills that is going to become so important for young learners to acquire in this new digital age that we have now entered, not just relative to mathematical competency, but in any number of different areas, simply because when a young person can identify these structural similarities within different areas of learning, it opens up all sort of possibilities for creatively relating them and for collaborating with others while doing so. That is, if a young learner is only able to see similar facts and ideas in two different areas of learning, but not similarities that might exist in the actual structures of those areas, then his capacity to creatively relate the two areas will not be nearly as great as that of someone who is able to perceive their analogous structures.

For example, a young learner who is able to apprehend how the structure of logical thought that she is using to prove different theorems while learning basic geometry is similar to the structure of thought she needs to employ to provide a proper argument and conclusion in a piece of expository writing on which she is working will have given herself an excellent working model for how to express herself properly on the written page. Likewise, another student who is learning how structural changes that take place in the human body as it grows and develops mirror changes that took place in the animal species itself as it evolved over millions of years, and is then able to identify similar structures of change that might be taking place in his own cognitive development as he matures, will very likely have provided himself with a real key to understanding how his own mental processes occur.

Furthermore, even if these students don't go on later in life to be writers or learning theorists, or even to deal extensively with geometry, journalism, evolutionary biology, or cognitive psychology, they still will have had the opportunity to identify and relate important structural similarities that exist in different areas of learning. Hence, when they do reach their adult years and enter the modern workforce, there is a genuine possibility that this same creative, relational thinking will still be a part of how they apprehend different problems and situations.

In large measure, digital pioneers like Bill Gates or Steve Jobs were successful because they were able to identify important structural similarities that exist between how a computer works and how people communicate and share information with each other; and even though their specific genius may have been something they developed apart from their academic learning, that doesn't mean we can't engender an analogous degree of creative thinking in today's students by providing them with learning environments that facilitate a similar apprehension of structural similarities that exist in different subject areas.

Yet in order to do this, we're also going to need to engender the ability in them to distinguish knowledge and information that necessarily exists in isolation from that which can in fact be creatively related to other knowledge and information, this being necessary if they're not going to inevitably waste time and energy wandering in a labyrinth of blind alleys that lead nowhere while trying to connect information and knowledge that necessarily exists in isolation to other facts and ideas. In addition, young people are going to need to increasingly learn to distinguish specifically what knowledge and information needs to actually be learned from that which can simply be retrieved on the World Wide Web whenever necessary. For example, learning the names and accomplishments of certain historical figures or the exact location of particular countries on a map would appear to be information for which it is no longer necessary that a student spend the same amount of time and energy that he once did committing to memory now that Google or some other search engine can immediately provide these for him. That is, these locations, names, and accomplishments are isolated pieces of information that one can instantly retrieve whenever one needs them.

On the other hand, learning something like the different parts of the human digestive system involves learning not only where a particular organ is located in the human body, but also comprehending that organ's function in relation to other organs. Therefore, simply retrieving the location of the kidneys or the liver through the Internet is not going to be sufficient to permit a student to understand how the digestive system works simply because in order to do that he is actually going to need to learn relevant functions and processes; particularly if he is going to be able to eventually relate this information to other information and knowledge, such as the effects that certain foods and medicines might have on his own body.

However, as one might imagine, there are also a number of different types of information and knowledge for which it is not so clear whether or not simple retrieval is going to be sufficient; and if students spend time and energy committing to memory facts and ideas that can simply be retrieved in order to be effectively utilized, they will have much less time to devote to learning how to creatively relate them, or to collaborate with others in doing so in preparation for the world into which they are moving as adults.

One such example of the type of information that might be open to question is the multiplication tables. That is, if a student is not able to easily memorize his multiplication tables, or else shows very little interest in doing so, does it make sense for him to spend a significant amount of time each day memorizing them when he can simply retrieve them on his computer or calculator any time he needs them? Or is memorizing the multiplication tables a skill that is not only essential to his ability to function optimally in the adult world, but also essential to his ability to understand how basic mathematics works?

This is the type of question that is going to need answering if teachers are going to have the time and latitude to assist students in developing unique learning progressions by creatively relating different facts, information, and subject matter. That is, how much of today's curricula in our schools, and indeed how much of the skills and knowledge that are presently part of the Common Core Standards Initiative, are areas of learning that can simply be retrieved on the Web, and how much must actually be learned if one is to become successful within a particular area of learning?

In addition, as the nature of any number of different occupations fundamentally changes in our new digital age, similar questions regarding the significance of different types of skills and knowledge are obviously going to need to be asked in greater depth. For instance, the profession of journalism has obviously undergone significant changes, particularly in terms of how rapidly the news of different stories and important developments travels around the globe. Hence, young people who might one day enter this profession are most likely going to need a vastly different set of skills that will allow them to do so. That is, as the newspaper industry becomes increasingly digital, and because news programs on cable television have now replaced the traditional half-hour evening news broadcasts as primary sources of news for most people, we not only receive news of significant events much more quickly, but also at the same time, events that are truly important are increasingly reported alongside far less important, sensationalized stories that are primarily designed to titillate viewers and increase ratings. Hence, as reports of news events arrive much more quickly on people's computers and television screens, and often occur alongside other events that are far less significant, young people who might one day be reporting those events, or even those who are simply interested in becoming informed citizens, are going to need a different set of skills from that which was previously necessary. More than anything, it would seem, they are going to need to learn how to quickly assimilate the essence of breaking news stories, relate those stories to other events that might be simultaneously transpiring, and likewise develop the capacity to view all stories within their larger context.

Yet when one examines some of the recent Common Core Standards for reading informational text for students in grades six through eight, it would appear that those who wrote them are still living largely in a twentieth century world in which people could digest the news much more slowly because of how it arrived through daily newspapers and network television. Included in these skills are the abilities to cite specific textual evidence to support analysis of primary and secondary sources, provide an accurate summary of the source distinct from primary knowledge or opinions, or identify key steps in a text's description of a process related to history or social studies. In other words, these are skills that have largely to do with analyzing, summarizing, or logically apprehending a particular piece of writing. And yes, of course, these are skills that have been and in fact still are valuable if one is endeavoring to slowly and carefully write or read a news story employing a logical analysis of its validity.

At the same time, however, there was seemingly little or no mention in the Core Standards of more relevant skills that seem important for young people to develop if they wish to learn to clearly read or write about significant world or national events in our current digital age either as journalists or as concerned citizens. These would be the capacity to quickly synthesize seemingly disparate facts centering around a single event into a coherent whole, the ability to ferret out bits of information concerning the event that has no genuine significance to its overall meaning, or the capacity to quickly relate the event to other events or trends that may be occurring simultaneously in different parts of the world.

In point of fact, this is the type of creative, relational thinking that is going to be important for students to learn as they approach adulthood or any possible career path in this new information age that we have now entered. At the same time, however, if lessons in various subject areas are to be presented more expansively to students in ways that allow them to develop this type of thinking by learning to perceive important connections and relationships, then it seems critical that these lessons are turned inside out, so to speak, so that knowledge and skills that students gain come at the end of the lesson, rather than at the beginning, as is the case in most schools today.

This means presenting information and knowledge to students in a manner in which, after being given a broad field of facts, ideas, historical references, and so forth, the students are asked to make their own creative connections within the particular learning area by answering a question that gets to the heart of what they are being asked to learn. For example, a group of students are learning about the different organs in the human body, specifically how they might affect one another. If the students are learning how the heart and lungs work together to pump oxygen rich blood through the body, how the kidneys work to eliminate wastes, or how the brain directs the central nervous system, and then are simply asked to learn these facts that have been taught to them within the context of a preconceived learning sequence, there is very little chance for them to develop the initiative to engage the subject creatively and relationally.

On the other hand, if they are given a broad field of information and knowledge related to the different organs and how they function, and are then asked to answer certain questions by attempting to perceive significant relationships and connections, then it becomes much more likely that they will develop the initiative to apprehend the subject area in unique ways simply because they are being asked to think more expansively about it. These questions could be along the lines of asking them to develop a basic hypothesis for how the organs in their bodies might be affected by the specific physical or social environment in which they live, or what they think the basic differences are in how particular organs of theirs function compared to those of their parents or grandparents.

As a result, by creating their own learning progressions toward the knowledge they are being asked to comprehend, the students are being given the opportunity to learn about the functions of the organs in their bodies from the inside out—that is, to determine these for themselves by endeavoring to discover creative ways to relate significant information and knowledge in answering a specific question pertaining to a broadly based subject area. Then, as a result of this, once they become accustomed to engaging areas of learning in this more indirect, creative manner, they will be able to do so more easily as they approach adulthood and enter into a global marketplace where the capacity to adapt to rapid changes in the workforce and to quickly relate seemingly different information, ideas, and knowledge have both become so vitally important.

As Tony Wagner, Innovative Education Fellow at the Technology and Entrepreneurship Center at Harvard puts it, "The world no longer cares how much you know. The competitive advantage comes with what you can do with what you know. Therefore, applying knowledge and creating something new from it—innovating—is what education has to be about."

One area in which this particular philosophy might be significant is the recent use of computer games to solve real-world problems; and how this trend might be effectively brought into the modern classroom. To this end, Jane McGonigal, a game designer with a PhD from the University of California–Berkeley, believes that one of the best ways to learn to fix many of our current social, economic, and political problems is by playing various computer games that address these issues. As an outgrowth of this belief, McGonigal has designed games for business, the arts, entertainment, social and environmental causes, and political movements.

Encouraging educators to use games to facilitate collaborative decision making among students so that they might come up with various solutions to all manner of real-world difficulties, McGonigal has been involved in launching games such as *World Without Oil*, an online game that challenges players to deal with the world's oil reserves online; *Evoke*, a social network game designed to empower people all over the world to come up with creative solutions to the world's most urgent social problems; and *SuperBetter*, a game backed by scientists that assists people in building personal resilience and a motivated, optimistic outlook by boosting physical and emotional well-being. There are also games such as LavaMind's *Zapitalism*, which employs beautifully rendered 3-D images and multiplayer functionality to give students of all ages experience in running their own business by learning how to buy and stock products based on key economic data; invest in a company's image; grow a business through successful maintenance, public service, advertising, and marketing; pay taxes and take out loans; determine salaries; buy insurance; and buy and sell shares of stock by investing surplus capital.

It is easy to see how classroom teachers might employ games such as *Zapitalism* or those created by Jane McGonigal to stimulate creative, collaborative thinking in their students relative to any number of different subject areas that can be easily related to real-world scenarios. In fact, Cathy Davidson, while researching her book, *Now You See It*, found a charter school sixth-grade class in North Carolina in which students take what they learn in their other classes, and then use that information, through playing various games, to come up with workable solutions to real-world problems while testing the validity of their solutions in real-world and experimental situations. They follow this by writing essays that document those results.

The question would seem to be this, however: Even if certain teachers are able to effectively employ various computer games in their classrooms to engender collaborative, relational thinking among their students, might much of this be undone if the remainder of the learning milieu in a particular classroom or school remains one in which information and knowledge flows vertically from teacher to students, and in which predetermined curricula and standardized testing shape both subject matter and classroom environments? Furthermore, will the ability to collaborate with others that students might learn while engaging in various online gaming strategies to solve important social, economic, or political problems related to specific areas of learning likewise be compromised when they return to classrooms in which they are not given free movement throughout the remainder of the school day, and are thus prevented from collaborating with their fellow students as fully as they might? And finally, if young people are to use tools such as computer gaming as effectively as they might in order to engender more creative thinking and learning, won't they first need to learn how to consider facts, ideas, and information in a larger context in which they can effectively relate them?

All of these questions would seem to be part of the larger question of how far technology can take us in engendering more creative learning in today's students in preparation for entrance into the current information age if the actual structures of classrooms aren't first changed to engender the ability in young people to approach knowledge and information creatively, relationally, and collaboratively.

The important skills for students to acquire in this new digital age that we have now entered are no longer what they once were in our former industrial age in which an increasing division of labor led to the need for schools to educate their students to assume increasingly specialized roles by assimilating highly specific knowledge and information. Now both the speed at which information is available to everyone and the sort of increasingly advanced tools that one can employ to access and use that information mean that schools need to make a point of educating young learners in how to think creatively in regard to any new knowledge or information that they might apprehend.

In this regard, one of the most important skills that will allow students to do this would appear to be the capacity to recognize specific types of relationships shared by different information within different subject areas. For once young learners begin to acquire this ability, their capacity to recognize significant relationships that might exist within a certain area of inquiry is soon expanded exponentially. That is, if a student can begin to recognize more quickly how certain facts, ideas, and knowledge relate to each other within a particular subject area simply because he has realized that this particular relationship is identical to one he has recognized earlier within a different subject area, then he is well on the way toward regularly employing the type of creative, relational thinking that will auger well for his future success in our current digital age no matter what field of endeavor he may choose as a career path.

For example, a student, after learning exactly how certain facts, ideas, and events within a specific historical period are related, could learn to look for the same type of relationships within a particular work of art or literature or within important scientific discoveries. Or she could even be presented with lessons in these different areas and then asked to identify specific relationships that exist between knowledge and information within all of them. To this end, she could actually be presented with specific exercises by her teacher that would allow her to develop this skill.

For instance, a group of middle or high school students could be presented with examples of how the breaking down of certain social barriers led toward the more informal relations between people, particularly between men and women, which took place within American society following World War II, and then learn to discern how the breaking down of similar barriers during the same time period led to a different apprehension of the fundamental principles of the atom in the world of science, or how a similar way of looking more informally at the relationship between impressions and reality took place in the art world vis-à-vis the abstract expressionists.

However, if such lessons and exercises in creative, relational thinking are to appear in the modern classroom, and to have genuine meaning to students there, then it is difficult to see how that will truly occur if current subject areas in most schools are not broadened exponentially to include one another.

In fact, integrated curricula are increasingly occurring in many schools today. According to an online article by Susan M. Drake and Rebecca C. Burns on the ASCD (Association for Supervision and Curriculum Development) website, "Meeting Standards Through Integrated Curriculum," an increasing number of schools and classrooms are employing several different ways to integrate subject matter. One is through multidisciplinary integration, in which specific disciplines, and their important skills and concepts, are organized around a specific theme or activity.

One example they use for this type of multidisciplinary learning is how eleventh grade students in Virginia explored the ecosystem of a local pond through a number of different disciplinary lenses of science (earth science, biology, chemistry, and physics), English (genre readings, analysis, and communication skills), and Math (data analysis tools and techniques)—with their teachers carefully connecting these activities to relevant standards of learning for each discipline. As mentioned earlier, there were also the fifth-grade students at a math, science, and technology academy in New York City learning the concepts of ratio and proportion by designing and constructing homemade kites, first on a computer and then using real life materials, while studying such diverse topics as electromagnetism or the use of kite flying in different cultural celebrations while learning the relevant mathematical concepts.

Of course, these examples of integrated curricula and subject matter are great ways for young people to learn to think creatively and relationally, and to collaborate with each other in doing so. However, it is also possible that these integrated activities will be less than successful in engendering this type of creative learning if they are essentially tied in any manner to either predetermined subject matter or empirical standards such as standardized test scores or grades put in place to measure such learning. For once the primary reason for integrating different areas of learning is so that students can achieve a greater measure of competency with a specific skill or absorb a particular piece of knowledge more effectively in order to meet some type of preconceived empirical standard, rather than for the purpose of learning how to creatively relate it to other areas or to the real world in which the students live, then the entire milieu in which those different relationships might be apprehended becomes immediately restricted by the student and teacher's need to focus on that upon which the students will be eventually evaluated.

One of the small group classes we held at The Children's School involved the study of different cognitive and developmental theories of human growth, particularly during a person's childhood years. Consisting of young people between the ages of eleven to fourteen years, the class studied the theories of Freud, Jung, Rudolf Dreikurs, and Jean Piaget in relation to both cognition and personal growth.

By far, the theory that had the biggest effect on our students was that of Piaget. Because the students were able to learn specifically how, according to Piaget, children and adolescents move, step by step, from concrete to representational to full abstract thought in conceptualizing their world, they were able to look into the mirror of their own evolving cognitive development. Consequently, they actually began, in many cases, to more carefully observe many of their own thought processes and perceptions of their immediate social environment.

However, what became just as interesting was to watch many of these older students then begin to observe the behavior of the younger children in the school in light of what they were learning about their own cognitive development. In fact, in a number of different instances, these older students even developed a certain degree of compassion for the younger ones as they began to comprehend that they were in fact operating on an entirely different cognitive level.

Almost certainly, if the students who had been a part of this class were aware that they would be empirically evaluated in some manner on what they were learning in regard to personal and cognitive development, they would have focused on the specifics of the theories they were learning rather than being so easily drawn toward a certain real-world application that was directly in front of them (i.e., the cognitive development of the younger children). In addition, because I taught the class without any type of predetermined approach or curriculum leading toward evaluation, the students were able to determine its direction based on seamlessly relating what they were learning about their own mental powers to different theories that concerned just that.

This is one example of why subject matters being integrated in a manner that stimulates the sort of creative, relational thinking that will serve to prepare students for the information age they will soon inherit necessitates that grading, standardized testing, and other empirical measurements shouldn't be allowed to become part of this process. For once they do, the focus of both the students and the teachers, when faced with the possibility of bad grades or unacceptable test scores, will soon be significantly narrowed in order to focus on the attainment of highly specific skills—to the exclusion of apprehending significant relationships and connections that might exist both within and between different subject matter, and in conjunction with their potential real-world applications.

IDEAS FOR REFLECTION

Once again, we are now living in a digital age in which the ability to perceive connections that others might not be able to see, to relate facts and information that might initially appear to be disparate, and to collaborate with others in pursuing both of these are rapidly becoming the new basic skills that are often more important than the attainment of highly specific skills and knowledge. Yet, at the same time, it is still vitally important for students to absorb many of the basic skills and much of the knowledge that will be keys to their future success.

Therefore, in light of this development, it would seem to be true that we need to implement a different type of accountability for students relative to how they attain significant basic skills and knowledge—an accountability that allows them to do so while employing the same creative, relational thinking toward different subject matters that is going to be so important for them to develop prior to entering the world of adult work and expertise that is now part of our current information age. That is to say, contemporary education may well need to move increasingly toward a place where the means by which young people absorb important skills, knowledge, and information will become even more important than that absorption itself. In fact, the ways in which students learn could easily become the new basic skills that our schools will need to implement. Of course, this particular idea needs more than a little explaining. Hence, it is the primary focus of the chapter that follows.

Chapter Four

Accountability and Initiative

Many people now have more opportunities than they did previously to become successful by proposing creative ideas and solutions to the world in the areas of science, technology, engineering, commerce, industry, or the arts—particularly now that it has become exponentially easier vis-à-vis the Web to cross what once seemed like impenetrable barriers dividing countries, societies, businesses, and occupations. Also, of course it is so much easier for someone working in a particular field of endeavor to access significant people working in the same field. Consequently, one now has the opportunity to immediately enter the global marketplace with one's creative ideas more fully developed and more viable than they might have previously been.

However, there is still the matter of initiative. That is, one can sit in the privacy of one's living room and dream up the most imaginative idea possible for a particular area of technology, industry, or commerce. Yet now that so many other people throughout the world are trying to do the very same thing, simply because they know how easy it has become to connect with others who might be able to assist them in turning their creative ideas into realities, those who will be successful at doing this will obviously be those who possess the most initiative.

In his book *How to Change the World: Social Entrepreneurs and the Power of New Ideas*, David Bornstein, the journalist and author who specializes in writing about social innovation, describes how people who are successful with new ideas that might solve major problems are relentless in pursuit of their visions—the kind of people who won't give up until they have turned their creative ideas into realities—and this heightened degree of initiative indeed has become the new standard for how to become a successful innovator in our current information age. Of course, now that the digital world has provided would-be innovators, particularly the young, with so

43

many new tools for organizing and coordinating their efforts, the need for a greater initiative in pursuing one's creative ideas is becoming increasingly profound.

So, in the highly competitive global marketplace in which we live, the question has to be asked: How does one facilitate the greatest degree of initiative in students who are being educated in our schools so that when they enter the information age as adults, this initiative will still be part of their makeup? And it would seem that in order to answer this question, one has to begin by carefully examining the intrinsic relationship that might exist between initiative and accountability.

In short, is there a way to fuse initiative with accountability so that students are in fact held more accountable for developing the initiative to explore certain subject areas and skills in creative ways that genuinely interest them, while at the same time, are held less accountable for simply meeting predetermined, adult-conceived standards of learning that the students themselves have had no hand in creating? Furthermore, for students in their elementary and middle school years, this question is particularly more difficult to answer than it would be for older students who have already acquired many of the basic skills and knowledge that they will need in order to face the world as adults. For in the case of these older students, it becomes exponentially easier to integrate initiative with accountability by holding them accountable for following through on creative approaches to learning, or for developing personal projects that will allow them to do so, simply because there is often no longer this issue of their needing to learn from scratch the basic skills that will assist them in becoming functional people in the world. However, for young students who are learning to read, write, work with numbers, or acquire essential knowledge about the world in which they live, the question of how they might do so while, at the same time, developing the sort of initiative that will remain with them during their formative years, in preparation for a world in which initiative has become increasingly important, becomes much more complex.

Today's teachers and younger students are being held increasingly accountable for teaching and learning basic skills and knowledge through the use of predetermined curricula and standardized test scores. Yet there is an obvious inverse relationship that necessarily exists between these two dynamics and the blossoming of initiative in young learners, the primary reason for this being that the need to produce higher test scores inevitably narrows the curriculum in classrooms as younger students are taught the knowledge, information, and skills on which they will be tested. As a result, there is less opportunity for them to develop the capacity to think creatively and relationally. In addition, not only is students' creativity being stifled when they are presented with a narrower field of information in which to learn various subjects (i.e., that which appear on standardized tests or are part of predetermined core standards), but also the possibility for the growth of their initiative as learners is inevitably being constricted as well.

Attempting to influence where young learners direct their attention through the use of highly preconceived curricula or standardized test scores is going to inevitably cause them to become acquainted with a particular subject matter on a more superficial level when they are compelled to direct their apprehension of it along a particular path in order to achieve a certain empirical validation of their learning.

Consequently, both the power and clarity of certain impressions that may have evolved from curiosities and interests of theirs that are genuine will almost certainly become dulled simply because those young people are not able to spend the requisite amount of time becoming absorbed in these relative to a particular area of learning. As a result, their initiative to pursue a subject matter in unique ways will inevitably be dampened when they are not given the opportunity to take those curiosities, interests, and impressions to a place of fruition.

During the time our school was in existence, there were a number of students who came to us after they had lost the initiative to learn in other schools, often primarily because certain aspects of their inner lives (i.e., their curiosities, interests, and strongly experienced impressions) had been so thoroughly ignored due to the results-driven approaches to learning that had been employed with them in those learning milieus from which they came. We were able to work with some of them to make a difference in their lives, while others we were not.

Yet in nearly all of these cases of students whose initiative to learn had been severely diminished, it became rather obvious soon after their appearance at our school that we needed to begin by dealing with the dynamics of their inner lives, rather than focusing primarily on academic subject matter and their successful cognitive apprehension of it.

One such student was a twelve-year-old boy who had been threatened with expulsion from his other school for a number of incidents of misbehavior. Normally, I might have been more skeptical about enrolling him. Yet, I knew his parents well, and a sibling of his had been a student at our school for a number of years. So I felt reasonably certain that I could communicate with the boy's family. After he arrived, those of us at the school soon found that assisting this young person in building a healthier inner life was not only the most important aspect of restoring his initiative to learn. It was in fact everything.

That is, because the strength of his impressions had been diminished, and his curiosities and interests had become so dulled in relation to his schooling, his initiative had taken the form of essentially trying to manipulate both the adults and other children in his world, rather than being directed toward what he might learn academically. Therefore, we began by simply trying to discover just what his genuine interests might be, and then moved from there toward not only assisting him in developing personal projects related to those interests, but also attempting to incorporate different aspects of these interests into other parts of his learning plan that we worked with him to create.

For example, he not only had a real talent for graffiti painting, but also a genuine interest in the social history and types of music that had spawned this particular art form. So we worked with him to design a learning plan that attempted to incorporate these interests into his efforts to become a better writer and more efficient reader, as well as working with him to design a course of study for the appropriate periods of American history that led toward the world of graffiti painting—the attempt we made in doing so, when seen in a microcosm, being a fairly accurate representation of the integral relationship that necessarily needs to exist between students' initiative to learn and the dynamics of their inner lives, especially as these two things relate to their future success in our current digital age.

In particular, this relationship seems relevant to younger students learning basic skills and acquiring fundamental knowledge in a manner that does not destroy their initiative—the best way to do this being to stimulate creative thinking and initiative in them while holding them accountable for absorbing important skills and knowledge in unique ways by simply wrapping the second around the first—that is, working with them to developing creative approaches to learning different subject matters and skills that facilitate their initiative, and then simply holding them accountable for not only following through on these, but for also working with their teachers to create even more unique approaches to apprehending whatever subject matter it is important for them to learn.

In other words, students would be held accountable for not only developing a curriculum that evolves from their particular interests relative to a specific subject matter, but for also actually creating the curriculum as it proceeds. The natural consequence for not doing so would be that if students are unwilling to put a certain amount of time and energy into developing this more creative approach, then their teacher is necessarily going to have to revert to developing the curriculum for them in advance. Hence their participation in a curriculum's genesis would be limited by the students' previous lack of effort.

For example, if a group of upper elementary or middle school students are learning about the United States Constitution, and how our court system implements it, they could be encouraged, in light of recent developments in our society, to begin by studying the issue of school shootings, gun control, and the second amendment—provided that this was what they were genuinely interested in pursuing. In addition, they could be allowed to consider such things as how the nature of their own classroom setting and how egalitarian it might be either does or doesn't mirror the rights guaranteed in the United

States Constitution. Their teacher could also suggest studying the constitutions of other countries, which they could download from the Internet, as a means of stimulating them to think creatively in developing their own approaches to learning about our bottom-line legal doctrine.

In other words, the teacher and students would simply work together to implement an approach that the students have developed, with there being a direct correlation between how much control the students have over how their acquaintance with a particular subject proceeds, and how much time, energy, and initiative they are willing to put into developing creative approaches toward it that genuinely interest them.

This different type of accountability, particularly when it proceeds without the narrowing of curricula by empirical test scores or national core standards, would be an effective way of facilitating initiative simply because students are not only given more responsibility for determining both the direction of their learning and the standards by which it will be judged, but also those standards in fact have a more organic relationship with students' direct experience of various subject matter. That is to say, the primary determinant of whether or not students are developing the proper amount of initiative to pursue a particular area of learning exists in their own efforts to connect their interests, curiosities, and strongly experienced impressions to the subject matter itself.

In 2009, three researchers from two different university departments of psychology, Piotr Winkielman and Lindsay Oberman from the University of California at San Diego, and Daniel McIntosh from the University of Denver, wrote in their study of embodied and disembodied learning of how modern embodiment theorists tend to see embodied learning as a goal-driven, flexible process that needs to work collaboratively with the more rote aspects of associative and rule-based learning. This means that for embodied learning (i.e., that in which students are fully emerged in whatever subject area they are apprehending) to effectively occur, the learner necessarily needs to incorporate the more fixed aspects of the knowledge he is attempting to assimilate into his own flexible, goal-driven approach.

This study is particularly relevant because of how it points to the fact that for younger students to learn necessary basic skills, while maintaining the initiative to do so because they are fully submerged in what they are attempting to absorb, it is important for their teachers to find a way to assist them in assimilating important fixed knowledge and skills in a manner that allows them the greatest degree of flexibility while doing so—meaning that although the fixed nature of certain significant aspects of the subject matter remains, at the same time those aspects also take place within a much larger context.

With this in mind, it may indeed be possible that the most significant negative effect of attaching standardized test scores and grades to a young person's learning is something far more severe than simply destroying her confidence with poor grades or low scores, although this can certainly occur. Rather, the real danger may be that these adult evaluations of student learning initiate an irreversible separation of the flexible, uniquely goal-driven nature of her personal experience from the more fixed nature of the cognitive learning in which she is engaged.

Consequently, much in the same manner in which a number of students at our school who had spent a significant amount of time in other schools where their learning was evaluated primarily by these types of empirical measures, and who then came to us when they were ten or eleven, often tended to keep what was occurring inside them separate from their academic learning, so the more rule-driven, rote nature of learning of basic skills, when disconnected from the curiosities, interests, and impressions of young people, can easily result in a dampening of their initiative to learn, even though they may not necessarily be able to articulate this particular frustration.

There was a particular ten-year-old boy who was enrolled in our school for a couple of years who had a number of genuine talents and interests, such as creating highly complex drawings with his colored pencils that approximated the sort of original, unique art found in many comic books. During the time he was with us, we attempted to assist him in integrating these interests into other academic skills, such as learning to become a better writer, and likewise worked with him to develop personal projects for one of our periodic project fairs through which he could demonstrate his ability in this area. Yet, unfortunately, because of his experience in other schools, which had so conditioned him to believe that what he learned at school and what fascinated him on a personal level had no genuine relation to one another, we were never really able to develop with him a program for academic learning that included, from its inception, his natural curiosities and interests. Often, I would observe him from a distance making his highly elaborate drawings in pen or ink at his desk, but was never really able to interest him in incorporating this particular skill into the rest of his learning plan. Unfortunately for him, the idea of school had become so entrenched in his mind as something that necessarily needed to be kept apart from his own interests and needs, that he had in fact erected a self-imposed barrier between the two so that the latter would never become diminished by the former.

That is why, particularly with younger children, it would appear to be so vitally important to develop learning progressions, subject matter, and curricula that begin with their inner lives, rather than developing them primarily as a means of engendering predetermined results. For once the latter process becomes a well-established pattern in their lives at an early age, the inevitable separation of personal experience from academic learning begins in many of them. As a result, it is easy to see how they can then become highly reactive toward their school experience, the result of this being that the opportunity to assist them in developing a genuine initiative to learn, or to follow through on their interests, often becomes significantly lost, never to be regained.

The educational researchers Karen Harris and Michael Pressley, in their 1991 revealing article, "The Nature of Cognitive Strategy Instruction: Interactive Strategy Construction," refer to how a number of contemporary cognitive scientists now acknowledge that, even while engaging in highly formalized subject areas, such as mathematics instruction, young learners who are successful often actively reconstruct the knowledge and skills they are attempting to acquire through new procedural forms, learning various shortcuts and the like. That is, as they develop proficiency, they do not do exactly what they have been taught, but instead often tend to personalize areas of learning they are attempting to acquire by actually transforming them.

This possibility that children who become successful learners often reconstruct the knowledge they are assimilating by personalizing it would appear to make it even more important that we find ways to fuse accountability for learning with the initiative to imagine knowledge, information, and even entire subject areas more creatively. For instance, if we had been able to engender a plan for learning in our school in which the ten-year-old student agreed to hold himself more accountable for finding a way to fuse his ability to draw with his efforts to become a better writer, then almost certainly we would have been more successful in engendering his initiative to learn.

This creative approach to engendering initiative by fusing it with a truer, more personal form of accountability in young people while they learn would appear to be one of the keys to preparing them for a digital age in which creative ideas or thinking are no longer enough if they are not significantly part of a certain level of initiative that allows the young person to see his or her ideas through to fruition. For example, one can imagine a student similar to our own who has developed a genuine artistic capacity during the course of his formative years, and as a young adult is able to imagine new, cutting-edge software that makes use of his unique artistic vision. Yet during his school years, there has been no genuine effort by his teachers to creatively incorporate his talent into a more expansive plan for learning for which he has agreed to become accountable. As a result, his initiative to develop his ideas, and to see them through in a practical manner, has likewise lain fallow. Therefore, when it comes time to introduce his unique visions to the digital world he now inhabits, he is more unprepared than he otherwise might be simply because, during the course of his formative years, he has not learned how to employ the initiative that he needs to employ in order to make himself successful.

David Bornstein writes in regard to modern social entrepreneurs who have made a real difference in the world that a good idea, even one that is masterful, is just like a play—one that needs both a good promoter and a good producer in order to open. In similar fashion, he writes that a good idea will not move from the fringes of the mainstream unless it is skillfully marketed. Otherwise it has no chance of changing people's perceptions or behavior.

Tony Wagner writes about an idealistic young filmmaker, Scott Rosenberg, who in 1991 in New York City began his program Art Start, a nonprofit whose purpose was to change the lives of at-risk youth by helping them to give voice to their ideas, visions, and stories through art that they would learn to create. In order to start his program, he found a last-chance city school that took students who had dropped out of or been expelled from other schools, and that agreed to let Rosenberg come in and teach a class in media and literacy.

Challenging the young people to look critically at various films that might appeal to them, such as the Hughes Brothers *Menace to Society*, the lyrics and music of rap artists such as Biggie Smalls, or various commercials, Rosenberg brought his idea to fruition by promoting it in a manner similar to that which David Bornstein alludes—that is, promoting it to the youth with whom he worked as a businessman addressing potential clients would promote his/her ideas to them. Consequently, Rosenberg approached the students with whom he worked as colleagues as he encouraged them to engage themselves in projects such as studying commercials, breaking them down, and analyzing them in order to understand how they did or didn't work, creating their own public service announcements as a team, or even visiting an ad agency and pitching their ideas about child abuse.

The type of creative initiative that drove Scott Rosenberg to inspire inner-city youth would be an obvious real boon to young people's efforts to eventually become successful with their own creative ideas in our highly competitive digital age. This is all the more so if it is successfully engendered within them during the formative years of their schooling, when there is a real opportunity to assist them in developing a focused approach toward their learning by actually holding them accountable for developing the initiative to absorb different subject matters by creating various unique approaches toward them.

Often, accountability and initiative become opposing forces in students that condition their experience. That is, students feel the weight of preconceived subject matter and standards of external accountability that they have had no real hand in creating, and so become conditioned to blindly accept them. While at the same time, they wish that they were given more time to pursue their own interests and curiosities, rather than having to be concerned with predetermined learning sequences or standardized test scores and grades. So very early on, students learn to equate the idea of being accountable for their learning with having their own initiative in pursuing what genuinely interests them stifled. As a result of this, many of them likewise become conditioned at an early age to view their own success as a function of simply pleasing other people, rather than as something that they creatively draw out of their own experience, this mental roadblock then becoming a genuine impediment to developing the sort of initiative that will lead toward their eventual success as adults in our current information age.

There have been numerous studies linking extrinsic rewards to a decreased level of initiative and perseverance in young students. In one significant 1999 study, educational researchers Deci, Koestner, and Ryan found that when schoolchildren of various ages received extrinsic rewards for participation in a task, they were less likely to participate in the task once the reward conditions were removed, although their levels of self-reported interest did not decline. What this particular study suggests is that extrinsic rewards offered students, while not having an immediate effect on their interests and curiosities, might actually dampen their motivation to continue with a task once the reward to do so has been removed, meaning that it's possible that the introduction of empirical evaluations of learning, such as grades or test scores, might inevitably lead toward a lesser degree of initiative in young learners than if they had never been introduced in the first place.

In their 2006 book, *Teachers, Schools, and Society, a Brief Introduction to Education,* education writers David Sadker and Karen Zittleman, write about the principal in a certain New York City middle school who decided to surreptitiously sneak extra mathematics learning into the curriculum in order to inflate math standardized test scores by having teachers who taught other subject areas, such as English or foreign languages, practice with their students how to correctly answer multiple-choice math questions similar to the ones that would appear on the test. As result, when the students learned that math scores mattered more to the people who ran their school than English or foreign languages, and when they fully realized that their classroom teachers were not the ones making the bottom-line instructional decisions, a number of students stopped attending school altogether, skipping the last five weeks of the school year. This would appear to be just one more example of the powerful negative affects that measures of external accountability, such as standardized test scores or grades, have on a dampening of students' initiative, and by extension, on their possibilities for becoming successful by bringing their creative ideas and thinking into the world they will soon inherit.

On the other hand, there is a different type of accountability that is more effective in stimulating initiative in young learners simply because it is more personal in nature. This would be one in which students have a direct hand in not only determining the standards by which their learning is to be judged, but in also deciding what the consequences will be for not becoming successful.

At our school in Evanston, each student had a lesson plan that he/she had negotiated at the beginning of the school year with the teachers at the school, with his/her parents in attendance. The lesson plan included basic skills that the student recognized he/she needed to learn, interests that he/she wished to pursue, different blocks of time that he/she had agreed to devote to particular subject matter, certain personal issues that the student wished to address, and the like. The plans were all kept in a large binder to which student and teachers alike could have immediate access.

At the end of the day, a teacher sat down with each student to determine if they had followed through on everything in their plan to which they had agreed to devote their attention.

If not, a specific consequence, one that had been decided by the students and teachers discussing the matter and then voting on it at a democratic meeting at which each child and each adult had one vote, was then equally applied to everyone. For example, one of the consequences that was voted into existence was that if a student had not completed everything on his plan the previous day, then he could not go out to morning recess the next day until he had.

In other words, students had a direct hand in determining the consequence for not doing what they said they were going to do, which meant that because this was discussed and decided vis-à-vis the full participation of all the students in the school, the consequence became entirely personal in nature simply because everyone fully understood its genesis; as compared to an external consequence such as a grade or standardized test score, which nearly always begins at some adult-conceived, bureaucratic place that young people can't possibly fully understand.

This different type of accountability is more effective in facilitating initiative in students than the sort of external standards that students have had no real hand in creating. For while the latter are primarily objective standards, empirical in nature, that usually have no direct link with the personal experience of the learner, the former, more personal standards are something entirely different. For with these, the student is not only given more responsibility for determining standards for his/her learning, but those standards in fact have an actual organic relationship with his/her experience of learning situations.

What this means is that something such as an empirical test score achieved on a standardized test, representing a student's knowledge or skill level regarding a particular subject matter, has little to do with the learning process itself that the student has undergone in acquiring that knowledge or those skills. While consequences to which a student or group of students have agreed after a thorough discussion of how they might be applied stem directly from a genuine understanding by the students of not only the nature of the learning environment itself, but also from an understanding of their personal responsibility in relation to it.

Just as significantly, this type of more personal accountability is entirely synonymous with how the forces of accountability and initiative transpire in our current digital world, one in which information now changes so rapidly. That is, now that knowledge that at one time might have seemed final is so rapidly transformed into other knowledge in order to make way for real-world applications, an understanding of the actual processes that led toward the emergence of various bits of knowledge has now oftentimes grown even more important than acquiring highly specific facts, ideas, and information themselves.

This is what is now occurring at Harvard University's Wyss Institute for Biologically Inspired Engineering, where scientific researchers, rather than being content to publish their ideas and results in journals and then move on to the next experiment, work at absorbing lessons from nature and then tweak them across different disciplines to create something entirely new by focusing on processes that lead toward real-world solutions more than dwelling only on conclusions.

For example, Wyss chemist Joanna Aizenberg discovered a new, nonstick material by observing the slick surface of the insect-trapping pitcher plant. Rather than simply writing up her results, she then went on to create permanent nonstick surfaces that could keep artificial walls free of insect infestations, prevent ice from adhering to airplane wings, and deter bacterial growth on medical devices that are continually in contact with body fluids.

In similar fashion, the institute's director, Don Ingber, borrowing from knowledge he had previously assimilated while taking a class in abstract sculpture, employed the architectural concept known as *tensegrity*, that in which the energy that is stored in a structure causes it to pop back to its normal upright form after it has been flattened out, in order to design a porous plastic disc that, after being filled with tumor-specific proteins and implanted under the skin, reprograms the body's immune system to attack tumors.

In other words, adaptable thinking across various disciplines has now become a new watchword for success in our current age as information and knowledge not only move so rapidly across academic and professional boundaries, but also so rapidly morph into other forms so quickly. That is, process appears to be rapidly replacing even the content of highly specific knowledge and information in significance.

Yet, at the same time, our methods of instruction today remain heavily results oriented, in which learning is judged primarily by national core curricula and standardized tests, the content of which doesn't begin to reflect the rate of change in our current global marketplace in so many different areas of endeavor. Therefore, curricula that are developed to engender the highest possible test scores or to rigidly follow core standards can easily become highly restrictive in a manner that often makes the rate of change occurring in society inaccessible to young learners. While, on the other hand, learning that is process oriented in a manner that connects students to areas of learning as a whole, rather than requiring them to become familiar with a particular subject matter by acquiring only isolated pieces of information, becomes a much better way to stimulate the sort of creative approaches to problems that scientists at places like the Wyss Institute regularly employ.

The best way to accomplish this is to assist students in developing their own learning progressions in apprehending various subject matters—progressions that will more fully connect students to whatever subject they are learning simply because there is a direct connection between a progression and their own curiosities and interests, because the particular area of learning won't have any artificial boundaries imposed upon it, and because the students' learning is always proceeding from the inside out.

This is exactly what occurred at our school when a group of students between the ages of seven and eleven began a project with me in which we attempted to construct—using an organic chemistry textbook, bags of gumdrops, and boxes of toothpicks—a specific section of the DNA molecule. In order to do so, we used the gumdrops to represent the different atoms present in each of the four chemical bases, and the toothpicks to represent the particular chemical bonds.

The students had all, each in their own way, been interested in how mutations might occur in humans that would cause someone to be born with six fingers, albino hair, or a predisposition to getting cancer. By following this original interest increasingly forward, using only the students' growing interest in a subject area that likewise grew increasingly larger and more complex as we proceeded, we eventually moved from learning how different types of mutations might occur in people and animals to how mutations might occur in the structure of someone's DNA. Then, after deciding to actually construct a section of DNA with our gumdrops and toothpicks, we soon found our way into such areas as the relationship between the structure of DNA and how inherited traits are passed on from parents to offspring, the nature of the chemicals that make up the four chemical bases in DNA, and how DNA is in fact stored in both human and animal cells.

IDEAS FOR REFLECTION

Involving students in the creation of their own learning progressions connects them to areas of learning as a whole, rather than causing them to become familiar with a particular subject matter in a more restrictive manner in which only isolated bits of information are connected to one another. On the other hand, when young people actually work to develop a path toward the particular knowledge they are assimilating, their understanding of the entire subject matter, and their recognition of significant relationships that might exist within it, grows ever more complete.

However, if this more process-oriented approach to learning in which students create their own learning progressions toward various subject matters in a manner similar to how experts from the world of adult work are now doing ever more frequently in our current information age is to come to fruition in our schools, then it seems more than a little obvious that the structure of classrooms themselves are going to have to change in order to allow this to occur.

In short, the inner lives of young learners are going to need to be allowed to find a place at the center of the modern classroom. Then working outward from there, curricula, daily schedules, and methods can be developed that engender opportunities for the sort of creative, collaborative thinking that has become the essential ingredient for success in our new age. Hence, a truer, more complete initiative to learn might be engendered. How specifically this might be accomplished is discussed in the two chapters that follow.

Chapter Five

A Proper Structure

More than anything, creative learning surely has to do with ferreting skills, information, and knowledge out of one's own experience by perceiving significant connections that exist within a broadly defined area. That is, if the knowledge is given to a student in advance, prior to him becoming familiar with all of the various relationships that either lead toward it, or grow out of it, then nothing creative, innovative, or new is really occurring. On the other hand, if he comes to the knowledge on his own simply because he has in fact been the one to connect the relevant dots, then he is learning creatively.

John Taylor Gatto, in his 2009 insightful book, *Weapons of Mass Instruction*, makes the point that true education, as opposed to schooling that embraces highly specific subject matter, tends to regard things in their richest possible context much as great scientists do who have come to understand that a cross-fertilization of various academic disciplines is one of the powerful drivers of scientific advancements. In this regard, Gatto might well have been speaking of James Watson and Francis Crick, who when they uncovered the structure of DNA, had to integrally relate the disciplines of organic chemistry and physics, even though neither was a bona fide expert in either subject.

In similar fashion, if the details of important scientific discoveries are given to students in advance, along with the experiments that led toward those discoveries, then those students are learning in a closed system. However, if they are instead asked to conduct variations of those same experiments, without knowing beforehand what the results will be, and then asked to determine for themselves what important scientific principles might be implied from their results, then they are in fact making all of the creative connections for themselves. Consequently, it could be said that they are learning from the inside out.

Yet as soon as teachers become focused on the external results of learning, rather than on the process by which various learning progressions are engendered, this more indirect approach toward acquiring knowledge, information, and skills tends to go right out the window simply because the specifics of what students are acquiring become immediately more important than the process of how that acquisition takes place.

In a 2006 research study concerning process-oriented learning conducted by David Hanson of Stony Brook University—SUNY, Hanson makes the point that five key ideas have emerged from current research in the cognitive sciences about how people learn. This research documents that people learn by constructing their own understanding based on prior knowledge, experience, skills, attitudes, and beliefs; following a learning cycle of exploration, concept formation, and application; connecting and visualizing concepts and multiple representations; discussing and interacting with others; and reflecting on progress and assessing performance. What all of these ideas about effective learning seemingly point toward is that it is a process of actively constructing for oneself the knowledge that one wishes to eventually absorb—knowledge that should necessarily come at the end of the learning experience. This we have known since the time of Piaget, who wrote repeatedly of how the child mentally reconstructs the world that he experiences in order to better assimilate it.

Yet, in our current desire for certainty that students will absorb specific knowledge, information, and skills that we believe will prepare them for the world they are about to inherit, we have created results-oriented structures for learning in our classrooms that in fact turn the natural learning process on its head—in so doing, robbing it of its essential, all-important, creative nature by focusing on predetermined outcomes, validated by various empirical standards. Thus, we have made it impossible for learning to occur in most classrooms in a more natural, indirect fashion.

George Dennison, in his wonderful book, *The Lives of Children*, which concerns a small private school on the Lower East Side of Manhattan in the late 1960s, writes of how learning situations can be organically structured when a natural order based on the needs of children and the natural (as opposed to unnatural) authority of adults is allowed to occur. This means that explorations of learning areas that teachers and students pursue together in a thoroughly open-ended, non-preconceived manner will automatically bring about a natural structuring of both the learning situation itself and the relationships that might occur between adults and children within that situation.

At our school in Evanston, we continually attempted to do this by matching the needs of the children in the school with our own natural authority and adult knowledge and expertise. For instance, in sitting down with our students to develop individual learning plans, we continually urged them to become accountable for pursuing what we perceived might be their natural interests and curiosities. For example, if we knew that a younger child had a particular interest in something because we had noticed her gravitate toward representations of it that were in the classroom, but we also knew that it was difficult for her to verbalize what this interest was, we tried to help her do this so that the particular interest could be put into a more concrete form in the context of her individual lesson plan.

Or if we perceived that an older child obviously needed to work on a particular skill, such as how to write coherent themes or complete sentences, but that he had no idea where to begin, we would negotiate with him until we had hammered out a coherent plan that we were confident he would have a bona fide interest in pursuing. For example, with one eleven-year-old boy, we developed a program for learning mathematics that originated with his interest in sports memorabilia cards, and all the resultant statistics that are inevitably part of them. For another younger child, we created a whole language program for helping her become a better reader that originated with her interest in creating her own unique board games.

On the other hand, as soon as a particular learning environment becomes fashioned to produce preconceived results, this type of organic structuring between children and adults becomes immediately impossible to implement simply because the specific milieu is now being constricted and shaped in order to produce those same results. Hence, the sort of organic structuring of a learning situation that might develop out of children and adults working together in an open-ended fashion as they naturally integrate a child's needs and the adults' knowledge and expertise becomes no longer feasible.

Along these same lines, organizational structures of businesses in our current digital age are occurring in a more organic manner in order that a business might have the correct amount of flexibility in reacting to commercial environments that can be unstable and unpredictable— something that is obviously occurring at significantly greater speed as the profound impact of computers and the Web, the increasing globalization of businesses, and the advanced sophistication of customers, when taken together, have added to the increasing unpredictability of a global marketplace in which today's businesses must operate. Consequently, rather than employ a traditional, top-down structure in which owners or high-ranking managers make most of the important decisions for an organization while lower-ranking employees usually have highly specific tasks that don't change much from day to day, many businesses now use a horizontal or flat structure, in which employees at all levels participate in decision making while tasks change frequently throughout the day; thus allowing information to flow freely throughout the company.

Certainly, this is the model applied at major Internet companies such as Google and Facebook. Indeed, flatter organizational structures such as these, those with fewer levels of management, encourage employees to take initiative without needing approval from multiple managers. In the words of Dana Griffin of Demand Media, an American social media company that operates online brands that specialize in articles and videos, "Instead of 'shifting the responsibility' up the management ladder, flat structures empower employees to take charge, help make decisions, and take responsibilities for the company's success."

Therefore if learning environments in our schools wish to more effectively prepare today's students for the nature and structure of the workforce they will be entering, it seems obvious that classrooms themselves must begin to mirror more completely the type of organic structuring that is now taking place within that global workplace rather than make that type of open-ended, collaborative structuring ever more difficult to achieve because of an overreliance on preconceived curricula and standardized test scores.

At The Children's School, if we had been subservient to adopting highly specific, preconceived curricula aimed at producing certain test scores, or national core curricula, we never would have been able to structure our lessons or environment in the organic, collaborative way that we did simply because the students' individual plans would have had to have been shaped in accordance with these external impediments—just as Facebook most likely never would have been able to adopt the flatter, more collaborative structure that it employs if it had become a publicly traded company subservient to its stockholders at its inception, rather than later after it was established. In other words, it seems that the dynamics of our digital age are now catching up rapidly with the improper, top-down structures for learning that we have been applying for years in our classrooms, a dynamic left over from the earlier industrial age in which a more mechanistic approach to running a business, that in which the lines of authority radiated from the top down from a central source, was translated in our schools into the form of a classroom teacher who selectively controlled the flow of information to her students.

Linda McNeil, Director of the Center for Education at Rice University, in her 2000 book, *Contradictions of School Reform: Educational Costs of Standardized Testing,* delineates how a school that is run as a bureaucracy, or is part of a bureaucratic system, is inherently in conflict with itself simply because while the purposes of a school should be aimed at nurturing children and equipping them with new knowledge and skills, an educational bureaucracy focuses on processing numbers of students through regularized requirements that are part of the goal of providing students and teachers with certain credentials that establish that specific types of learning have taken place. McNeil goes on to suggest that a bureaucratic approach to education, which she likens to a factory, is tightly organized, highly routinized, and geared for the production of uniform products, while educating children is necessarily a complex, inefficient, idiosyncratic, uncertain, and open-ended endeavor.

Hence, once again, a bureaucratic school is by nature in conflict with the essential dynamics inherent in educating children in their formative years.

Of course, the primary agent by which schools inevitably become part of a highly bureaucratized system is through the use of standardized test scores to evaluate both the learning of students and the capability of teachers, and likewise the use of core curricula that are put in place to establish predetermined subject matter. For without this testing and those core standards, the tentacles of bureaucratic control would be unable to enter either individual classrooms or the lives of the students within them to the extent that they now do; until they wrap themselves entirely around the milieu of the modern school.

Therefore, if we are to begin to structure classrooms so that they are synonymous with what is transpiring within the worlds of professional expertise and business, we need to first remove standardized testing and national core curricula from our schools, replacing them with a new, truer form of accountability, and then attempt to structure the modern classroom from the inside out, beginning at the point where the actual needs of students meet the natural authority and knowledge of adults. Then proceed from there to develop milieus for learning that allow for the same organic, collaborative environments to flourish that are taking place in today's global marketplace.

In addition, because of the manner in which the old barriers separating businesses, countries, and workers are now being tumbled because of how connected the entire world has become, occupations that had once been highly specific are now being rapidly absorbed into other occupations, or else entirely eliminated. Consequently, it has now become more important than ever that students become the sort of creative, adaptable learners who will be able to move smoothly and efficiently between occupations when they are adults. That is, as job creation and elimination become increasingly speeded up in Tom Friedman's flat world, the individual worker is going to have to become increasingly adaptable in order to succeed.

Therefore, if students during their formative years are taught to develop a narrow, limiting approach to subject matter they are attempting to absorb, rather than being taught to perceive information, facts, and ideas creatively and expansively, then this same narrow, limiting approach is going to likewise become part of their adult mind-set. Consequently, it is going to become more difficult to reverse this trend as they approach adulthood; thus leading toward their becoming less creative learners and workers as adults.

In a very real sense, the sort of worker of who can easily adapt to changing conditions in the current global marketplace originates in young people's formative years. So one of the biggest challenges for the contemporary school is how to develop organic, collaborative classroom structures that facilitate creative, adaptive learning by expanding subject matter in the broadest manner possible—which means, once again, that restrictive dynamics that inevitably narrow subject matter, such as standardized testing or national core curricula, are going to have to be eliminated and replaced with those that actually allow for broad curriculum expansion.

One approach to expanding subject matter, in addition to the types of interdisciplinary integration of curricula mentioned in an earlier chapter, is integration of whole subjects into other, more expansive subject areas. To this end, some examples of integrated curricula for secondary school students were provided recently by experienced teacher Melissa Kelly on the About.com website. These were such things as combining world history and geometry in studying Greek civilization, mathematics and art/art history in learning about the design of cathedrals, biology and statistics while studying genetics, psychology and geography in apprehending urban planning, and literature and history/government in reading Ralph Ellison's great book from the Civil Rights era, *Invisible Man.*

Indeed, if teachers were actually held more accountable for stimulating this sort of creative, integrated learning in their students in the same way that they are now held accountable for their students' learning the specific facts and skills on which they will be tested, then our classrooms and schools might actually be said to be better preparing students for the rapidly evolving information age that they will soon be entering.

One way that teachers can do this is to make a point of introducing areas of learning to their students in a manner that enables them to discover the relationships that are implicit within them and between them, rather than focusing so much on subject areas as sets of isolated facts, ideas, and skills— a focus that obviously prevents students from developing a more expansive apprehension of what they are learning. For instance, in combining basic biology, particularly genetics, with beginning algebra, teachers could use their pupils' understanding of how basic set theory works to design lessons that incorporate this understanding with how the different chemical bases align themselves with each other in the structure of DNA. Or the teaching of world history for the twentieth century could be tied to changes in global weather patterns that produced certain natural disasters, similar to the 2005 tsunami in Indonesia, which then produced certain economic, social, or political changes.

Then, when students reach adulthood, this same relational thinking can be employed to visualize certain self-organizing, collaborative communities with whom they might connect on the Web to facilitate their particular life's work. Or the capacity to realize similar relationships within different subject areas is the same capacity that can be used later, when one enters the adult workforce, to comprehend how developments in the world of computer-driven technology might be employed in the arts or the business world.

However, at the same time, it would appear to be most important that, after introducing subject matter within this larger context, or even instructing their students in how they might do so, teachers allow them to make all the relevant connections for themselves. Otherwise, the type of creative, relational thinking that teachers are attempting to engender will inevitably become just one more preconceived learning path that students are instructed to follow, something that does nothing to engender more creative learning.

The key, of course, is creating subject areas that are broad enough that students can themselves perceive the relevant connections within them, but not so broad that they begin to flounder in a labyrinth of facts, ideas, and information that seemingly have no connection to each other. In order to do this, it might be well to take a page from how experts who are currently successful in bringing innovative ideas to the global marketplace have adjusted the scope of their ideas in order to bring to fruition the most creative, workable ones.

Tony Wagner, in his extremely insightful book, *Creating Innovators, The Making of Young People Who Will Change the World,* writes of how when Apple developed the iPhone, they wanted a display that went almost to the edge so that the phone would look magical. However, doing this was enormously difficult simply because glass can break from preexisting microcracks in the edges. Yet in order to have a strong display that went right to the edge of the phone, the designers at Apple knew that they had to have really clean edges.

So immediately they began to work with those in their supply chain to understand how they could make cleaner cuts in the glass, even though this fine-tuned glass cutting had not previously been an aspect of their business. But then they began to realize that the display of an iPhone whose glass went almost to the edge could be impacted if it was dropped. Hence, after researching the matter, the solution became putting stainless steel around the rim.

In other words, the designers at Apple possessed a larger vision for their product, one that involved workers making parts that one would not normally associate with building a mobile phone. Yet, at the same time, they were acutely aware of the highly specific conflicts that inherently existed within their vision, and of the particular parameters within which those conflicts took root. That is, their approach to developing the iPhone evolved from creative thinking that was, at one and the same time, broad enough to bring something entirely new into the marketplace, but specific enough to allow designers to apprehend the important relationships born of conflict that existed within their endeavor.

In similar fashion, if subject matter within our schools were specific enough that significant learning could take place within various subject areas, but at the same time expansive enough that young learners could apprehend important relationships and connections that inherently existed within those expanded areas of learning, then classroom learning might begin to more closely approximate the world of connected, collaborative, highly creative endeavors that have in fact become keys to success in our current digital age.

Yet this more expansive approach to subject matter is forever at the mercy of the type of relationship that a classroom teacher has with her students. If the teacher tightly controls the flow of information and knowledge to her students as they sit immobile while they learn, then it is hard to see how subject areas could be expanded in any significant way simply because expanded areas of learning necessarily imply that students are actively involved in their creation, meaning that students be allowed to not only negotiate how particular subject areas might evolve, but also that they be given free movement throughout the day in investigating them.

One of the classes that took place at our school involved learning about modern architecture by creating structures with Legos, using pictures and diagrams of various examples of modern architecture from around the world as models. If we had decided to take these lessons to the next level by fusing them with lessons in basic geometry in order to create a larger, integrated area of learning, we could never have done so effectively if our school had been one where the teacher controlled the flow of subject matter to students who sat immobile at their desks.

Rather, we would have had to allow our students to have a hand in deciding what particular forms of architecture engaged them relative to their abilities in basic geometry. They also would have had to have been able to move back and forth freely between the Lego structures that they were constructing and the geometric principles that they were apprehending in attempting to build those structures more effectively. Otherwise, it would have been impossible for them to develop a genuine connection between basic geometric principles and their immediate application of them in the form of their Lego constructions.

This is just one example of why expanded, integrated areas of learning necessarily imply a certain structure for learning that will allow them to properly evolve. Otherwise, specific structural boundaries, such as preconceived curricula, student immobility, or a teacher who employs unnatural adult authority with his students will inevitably become barriers to expansive, integrated subject matters.

In addition, teachers who continue to teach in a manner in which they simply give their students knowledge and information in advance and then hold them accountable for learning it, as most teachers in most classrooms now do, tend to adopt a very different role with their students than they would if they set up lessons so that their students could instead draw their learning out of their own experience by creating unique paths toward particular subject matter. Essentially, the difference has to do with the teacher relating to her students as receivers of information and then teaching them accordingly, rather than relating to them as active, coparticipants whom she is attempting to empower to develop their own learning progressions.

In the first instance, the role of the teacher in relation to her students is almost entirely vertical in nature. That is, facts and information flow from the top down to her students in a manner in which the teacher controls that flow; whereas, in the second instance, the teacher's relationship with her students is more horizontal in nature. This means that she is essentially neither an exclusive possessor of significant facts and information within various subject areas, nor somebody exclusively in control of their transfer to her students. Rather, her role is one of presenting those facts and information in a manner that will stimulate her students to become acquainted with these by discovering ways to turn them into their own utilitarian knowledge.

Yet, once again, for teachers to work with students as equal partners in creating workable learning progressions of which students are in direct control means of course that the learning environment is necessarily going to have to be structured in a manner that will allow this to occur. One place that educators might look in attempting to apprehend such a non-hierarchical approach toward creative learning are innovative companies in the current global marketplace who have developed their own adaptable, creative, and collaborative structures that allow employees to become genuine participants in the evolution of the company.

Looking at the flat structural hierarchies that exist at software giants like Google and Facebook, it becomes immediately apparent how different they are from the exclusively top-down hierarchies that presently exist at a number of other large companies and businesses. At Google, there is the opportunity for workers to communicate ideas freely and immediately with not only those who work at the same level, but also directly with those several levels above them, without having to push their ideas up the chain of command, so to speak, in the manner that has previously existed, and continues to exist, at most major companies.

Software engineers and others work together in small teams with each person on the team getting to touch each aspect of a project, creative ideas being far more important than job titles. That is to say, the ability to drive and participate in innovation at Google is not limited to a select few PhDs working in their research labs. Rather, it is open to all employees. The company not only believes that innovation can unexpectedly come from any employee at any time, but that such innovation is actually expected of every employee.

Although Google of course has a traditional job ladder with familiar titles, it has always tried to keep the ratio of individual contributors who might become creative to managers as high as possible, with it not being unusual for thirty or forty people to report directly to a manager, and with the key role of managers to guide and connect, not control. In this regard, Google says it is even willing to accept a certain amount of chaos as being not only the price they pay for innovation, but in fact one of the necessary ingredients for innovation.

In addition, the company's paper-thin hierarchical structure is one of the reasons it is able to attract so many of today's talented young people, who have grown up in an age of egalitarian information sharing and instant connections to people of stature around the globe, as future employees. They like the flat organizational structure that allows them to be both more creative and more collaborative in ways which they have become used to in our current digital age.

While at Facebook, it would seem, this typical, often inhibiting, top-down hierarchical structure has likewise been largely eliminated; with egalitarian communication between workers resembling the lines and black dots that exist on a soccer ball. That is, there is the opportunity for immediate and direct communication with pretty much anyone in the company, all the way up to CEO Mark Zuckerberg himself. In fact, Zuckerberg has made the point on numerous occasions that the immediate, nonhierarchical sharing of ideas at Facebook has been a major factor in engendering the flow of creative ideas that steadily takes place there.

Recently, noted educators such as education historian Diane Ravitch and Randi Weingarten, the President of the American Teachers Federation have traveled to Finland to observe the structure of their highly successful schools in hopes of bringing new ideas to our country's endeavors to better educate its students; and of course this is all to the good. However, it might also be argued that excellent structural models for how classrooms in our society might better prepare students for the world they are about to inhabit already exist right here in the United States at modern software companies like Google and Facebook.

Indeed, this might lead toward classroom structures similar to what we endeavored to achieve at our school in Evanston—that is, ones in which learning necessarily emerges from a web of egalitarian relations that exists between teachers and students, with everyone having both equal rights and equal responsibilities relative to both their learning and their relationships with each other. In such structures, there is ongoing, open-ended, egalitarian sharing of any information, suggestions, or ideas that will not only improve the learning environment in general, but also the learning and healthy personal development of the individual students within that environment.

Every learning or social situation that occurs in any classroom necessarily possesses inherent rights and responsibilities that are part of the situation itself. That is, there is a certain equilibrium in any situation in which the specific rights and responsibilities of those involved, both teachers and students, need to be in balance with one another if the students in that classroom are to experience themselves as being fully connected to the learning environment itself. Otherwise, when students experience that their rights are not in balance with those who teach them, or with other students, it becomes very easy for them to begin to withdraw, both mentally and emotively, from learning situations in which they find themselves.

Therefore, it would seem, a real key to creating the type of open-ended, collaborative learning communities similar to what are now transpiring in the global marketplace would be to begin by endeavoring to recognize generally what rights and what responsibilities students and teachers necessarily have in relation to one another. For example, how much say should students have in how their curriculum evolves or in determining the standards by which their learning is judged? Or how much input should they be given in terms of how their school day is structured or in how they want their teachers to instruct them?

Many of these are fundamental questions that are either partially or fully ignored in the vast majority of our schools today. That is, it doesn't occur to many educators to give their students a genuine hand in determining curricula, standards for evaluating learning, the daily classroom schedule, or the manner in which they feel they need to be instructed if their learning is to evolve in an optimal manner. Yet this is very much the dynamic that is occurring in many modern workforce environments, particularly the most innovative ones. That is, workers are being given a much more direct hand in how day-to-day decisions at a particular company evolve, particularly as many companies are beginning to realize that there is a growing disconnect between the increasingly flexible networks for personal communication that we now all enjoy in our present digital age and the rigid, hierarchically structured environments in which many people still work.

A number of businesses, however, are in fact rising to the challenge of this changing dynamic. For instance, Proctor and Gamble's Clay Street Project has created multi-disciplinary teams that focus more on market needs than on the performance of different divisions within their company. IBM has developed Beehive, an organization-wide network of idea sharing designed to facilitate employee contributions. And AT&T's Innovation Pipeline, aimed at giving employees at all levels within the company a chance to have their ideas heard, has already significantly changed the company's formerly hierarchical structure to one that is now more egalitarian and collaborative.

IDEAS FOR REFLECTION

If the modern classroom is to be structured in a manner similar to how contemporary businesses and companies are increasingly structured so that young people will be more prepared for entrance into these as they reach adult life, then our classrooms must necessarily become more collaborative and egalitarian. However, this is not going to occur unless two fundamental relationships change first. One is the actual relationship that students have with the information and knowledge that they are assimilating. The other is the nature of the relationship between teacher and student. And because both of these relationships are integrally tied to one another, it would seem that they must both change simultaneously.

That is to say, the idea that facts, information, and skills should be seen as utilitarian tools that students employ to learn creatively, rather than as things that their teacher selectively passes on to them and then asks them to learn in isolation from each other is really at the heart of how the role of the teacher must change so that young people might learn more creatively, adaptively, and collaboratively in preparation for the world they will soon inherit. For such learning is something that can simply not be force-fed to students. Rather, it can only be engendered by teachers setting up conditions in their classrooms in which their students have the correct relationship to what they are assimilating.

In other words, there is an integral relationship between the structure of a classroom, the relationship that evolves between student and teacher, and how students approach various subject matter. If information and knowledge resides essentially in the hands of the teacher and flows vertically to students who passively absorb it, then the students' relationship with their teacher and with their fellow students will be less collaborative, and the subject matters that they learn will inevitably become more constricted. On the other hand, if information and knowledge is experienced by the learner as being essentially his/her property, and flows horizontally from teacher to students who are active participants in determining how they will apprehend it, then those students' relationship with everyone in their learning environment will be more collaborative and subject matter will be engendered that will be able to grow organically as they become more expansive.

Yet if today's students are going to become the sort of creative people who can adapt to the incredible rate of change that now takes place in our digital age, they will need to develop the ability to create their own paths toward apprehending various subject areas in a manner that remains with them as they grow toward adulthood in a world in which the present is turning into the future at an ever increasing rate. In order to do so, they are likewise going to have to develop a different type of relationship to information and knowledge itself, and simultaneously with those who teach them. This then is the focus of the chapter that follows.

Chapter Six

Teacher and Student

The manner in which knowledge and information now change so rapidly and so fluidly in our current digital age, it would seem, is going to produce the need for a different type of relationship between teacher and student—one in which the two might explore together how a young person can best learn specific facts, idea, and skills within such a fluid, constantly changing world vis-à-vis the teacher and student exploring together the world of adult expertise that is taking place outside the schoolhouse door.

For example, as was mentioned earlier, it was recently discovered that whereas previously genetic researchers thought that only about 2 percent of human DNA led toward the growth of cells and viable organs, it is now known that 80 percent of DNA has some biochemical function. Therefore, a middle school biology teacher and a group of students, working together, could explore the implications of this new piece of knowledge for human health and heredity. That is, the curriculum could actually become one in which teacher and students attempt to determine what implications recent developments from the world of biochemical research have for what they are learning about human biology.

Likewise, as was also delineated in an earlier chapter, when scientists discovered the long-sought Higgs boson particle at the Hadron particle collider in Switzerland, they simultaneously proved that there is indeed an energy field surrounding each of us which creates the matter of the world in which we live. Therefore, a high school physics teacher could use this development to explore with his students the ways in which it might change how human beings harness and then use various forms of alternative energy.

In the same vein, the three boys who learned theoretical physics with me at our school might have explored the discovery of the Higgs boson particle in an attempt to determine how this discovery might affect the validity and/or implications of Einstein's famous equivalence principle between matter and energy that we had studied together, or else possibly conjectured about what types of particles the Higgs boson might be composed.

In all three of these cases, there would be a genuine attempt by teacher and students working together to integrate a curriculum by focusing on events that are occurring in the world outside the schoolhouse door. In other words, as those external events change, so does the curriculum, and possibly also so does the nature of the relationship between teacher and student, as teachers become either more or less intrusive in presenting advanced subject matter to students based on the degree of interest and participation the students exhibit in accessing developments in the world of adult work.

This would also mean, of course, that classroom teachers would have more of a responsibility than they already do to make themselves aware of changes that are occurring in the world of adult work and expertise that might relate to what they are teaching so that they can then effectively involve their students in constructing subject matter and curricula that are based on those changes. For example, middle school science teachers might research the effects that new discoveries concerning the increased function of DNA might have for the field of biological science as a whole, or high school science teachers might research what effect the discovery of new particles might have on the study of physical science.

In addition, these perceived changes would not necessarily stem exclusively from changes occurring in the more obvious fields of physical and biological sciences, and of computer technology—three disciplines in which almost daily changes are now occurring. The worlds of journalism, geographical boundaries, the application of mathematics as it relates to computer coding, and the visual arts as they relate to applications in our current digital world are all undergoing significant transformations as well. Hence, subject matter corresponding to developments in those particular areas, in addition to that of the sciences and computer technology, might likewise undergo certain transformations, as was alluded to in an earlier chapter.

As a result of this, one of the primary responsibilities of the classroom teacher might increasingly become one of involving his/her students in shaping subject matter in accordance with what is occurring in the world outside of school. That is, as changes occur more and more rapidly in specific disciplines in the modern world of work, teacher and student, working together, could shape the student's curriculum in accordance with those changes; both so that a student's learning is more relevant, and so that his thinking grows more flexible and adaptable in preparation for the world of rapid change that he is about to enter.

In other words, as information and knowledge from the world of adult expertise changes more rapidly, there will be an ever-greater need for subject matter related to those changes to become more malleable, and for teachers to become more open and adaptable in their approaches to areas of learning in order that the subject areas they teach continue to remain relevant to changes occurring outside the schoolhouse door.

For example, now that print journalism, which appears these days increasingly online rather than in newspapers, is being condensed into the ever-smaller packages of information that have become the modern news report, and because of the speed by which both the Internet and cable television can report recent developments, there would seem to be a real need for those young people who are learning how to write cogent essays and who might possibly eventually become journalists or writers themselves, to learn how to condense their writing in a manner in which they can expound on what they have to say more succinctly than what previous generations of students were required to do.

Therefore, teacher and student could explore together breaking stories and news reports online with an eye toward the student's learning how to write as succinctly as possible in preparation for the world he is about to enter. Not only would the teacher be responsible for providing direction in examining the nature of writing in the current digital age, but the student could also become an equal participant by researching stories and other pieces of information online that truly intrigue him, and then sharing with his teacher his opinion of how those are written. In response, the teacher could then assist the student in writing essays in which he develops a cogent approach similar to the stories he has researched on the Internet.

In other words, by researching changes that are occurring in the world of professional expertise, and then applying those changes to how various subject matter might evolve, teacher and student would be working together to create a curriculum that evolves directly from what is transpiring in the world outside of school. Hence, the student would be learning in a manner in which he directly connects himself to the world he will one day inherit.

During the time our school in Evanston was in existence, as part of a class we had developed, a group of our older students explored together the legal system, the courts, and the United States Constitution. A significant part of that class involved journeying downtown to the federal building to observe various civil trials, or to the criminal courts building on the near South Side of Chicago to observe criminal trials. Needless to say, actually observing high profile civil suits or trials relating to serious criminal charges left a profound impression on some of our students relative to what they were studying.

Probably as much as anything, the students were able to observe both the degree of specificity with which both civil and criminal trials are conducted and the severe implications that legal trials can have on the people involved in them. In fact, on one occasion our students witnessed a sentencing hearing, complete with victim impact statements and closing arguments, in which a young man was sentenced to a long prison term for kidnapping and armed robbery. The next day, after we had returned to school and were once again conducting our class, there was of course much discussion concerning what our young people had witnessed that day.

In fact, actually witnessing in concrete detail what transpires during serious legal proceedings gave a new slant to what our students were learning about the law and the Constitution in our society. More than anything, I think, when we began to conduct our own mock trials together, these experiences caused them to more carefully consider both the ramifications and the detailed nature of legal proceedings.

Except for the possible development that sentences for criminal offenses might be handed down more harshly these days in Chicago due to the crime wave that has been sweeping parts of the city during the past ten or fifteen years, there were no real changes in the law being enacted that directly affected the trials our students observed during their time in either civil or criminal courts. Yet if the law for a particular area of litigation had in fact been in dispute, and thus in the process of changing, during any of the trials we witnessed, our students would have been given a great opportunity to connect their learning concerning the law directly to changes that were transpiring in the world outside their school, and thus they might potentially have been involved, provided they were given the proper amount of direction from myself as their teacher, in creating a curriculum based on those changes in the manner discussed above.

In similar fashion, another group of students at our school began journeying on a somewhat regular basis to the lab of a physicist at DePaul University. One of the best things he demonstrated to us, and one that completely absorbed the young people, were the different laser beams he was able to show us in operation, afterward teaching us how the different chemical properties that scientists have discovered as being part of the laser beams determine their color, size, and other characteristics. Obviously, this is another ever-changing field, this one involving physical science, which if studied by teachers and students working together, could easily lead toward the creation of ever-changing, fluid curricula emanating from the world of science outside the schoolhouse door.

Parenthetically, there was also the time the three boys who were learning theoretical physics and I attended a lecture together given by Stephen Hawking at McCormick Place on Chicago's Lakefront. The subject of the lecture, the nature of imaginary time, was enhanced by any number of colorful charts and pictures appearing directly behind Mr. Hawking as he sat on stage addressing the audience vis-à-vis the synthetic voice on the computer that was attached to his wheelchair. The following week the three boys and I attempted to incorporate, as best we could, this cutting edge development from the world of physical science, the idea of imaginary time, into what we were learning about the world of physical science.

In a similar vein, in his wonderfully engaging book, *Holler If You Hear Me: The Education of a Teacher and His Students,* Gregory Michie writes of how he conducted a class in media studies with a group of eighth-grade students at the public school where he taught on the South Side of Chicago, one which involved his students' learning how they might critically examine how the media presents stories to them, particularly those that emanate from the actual neighborhood in which they live. At the same time, they learned how to ferret out the messages that were being delivered to them by the television shows they watched.

More than ever now, this particular type of endeavor could be expanded upon in schools everywhere, that in which students and teacher work together to develop a curriculum based on recent changes they perceive occurring in the mass media, with visits to newspapers, radio and television stations, and other media outlets occurring on a regular basis. At the same time, the students could be examining how television shows are now exponentially changing, particularly now that cable television provides more serious, fully-developed, and better-produced shows than ever before. The goal of both of these endeavors would be for students to develop their own fluid subject matter concerning media studies based on what they observe presently transpiring in the world of the media with which they are familiar.

At the same time that these connections between school and the world of professional expertise are occurring relative to curriculum development, the relationship between teacher and student would seemingly need to become much more malleable in response to changes occurring within the world of professional expertise. For example, a middle school student who is more savvy about how important information is transmitted in the digital world than her teacher might actually be in a position where she could take the lead in researching how her lessons as a writer proceed, even as her teacher takes the lead in teaching her many of the technical abilities she needs to develop in learning how to write.

Likewise, as the need to learn to write computer code becomes ever more significant, different skills in mathematics and algebra that are related to coding are going to become increasingly important for students to acquire in preparation for the world they are about to inherit. Therefore, just as the need to learn how to write more succinctly and cogently might stem from the manner in which the modern news story is reported, so the acquisition of specific mathematical and algebraic skills might stem from how the increasing need for people to learn to write computer code applies to their particular profession.

Therefore, in a manner similar to how teacher and student might explore how the modern news story evolves online, or likewise changes in the worlds of legal proceedings, physical science, or the media, they could research together the significant part that computer coding now plays in various professions, and exactly what type of coding skills have become most important to acquire. Then out of that they could design a curriculum in mathematics and algebra that both believe best prepares the student for the world of professional expertise that he will one day enter, particularly in terms of the student's specific interests.

In addition, just as the relationship between student and teacher who were working together to help make the student a better writer grows more malleable relative to changes occurring in the worlds of journalism and writing, so might the relationship between a teacher and a student who is learning algebra and mathematics. That is, it is highly possible that the student, because he is savvy about the digital world, might be more informed about how computer coding might be applied there than his teacher would. Hence, he would tend to take the lead in this particular aspect of his particular curriculum, while his teacher would of course take the lead in teaching him the actual skills of mathematics and algebra.

Once again, in both of these instances, teacher and student working together to create a specific curriculum based on their research of changes occurring in the rapidly evolving world of professional expertise tends to create a more malleable, workable relationship between the two of them than what occurs if the teacher simply determines a learning path for a group of students in advance of their participation in its genesis.

As things stand now in the vast majority of our schools, educators develop curricula out of their own preconceptions of what skills, information, and knowledge it is important for students to acquire. Or else, as now is increasingly the case, educators develop curricula by referring to national core standards that a committee of researchers and educators have determined are important for students to meet at various levels of their education.

Yet one has to ask, how much time is actually taken by educators working in individual schools, or by those developing core standards, to actually research what effect specific changes occurring in the world of adult work might have on the development of curriculum in various schools so that learning there is more relevant to what might be occurring outside the schoolhouse door? Likewise, one has to ask how educators can somehow include students more fully in the determination of standards for their learning so that those students might come to feel that they are more in control of their own education.

Also, as anyone who has spent much time around today's young people already knows, they tend to be more savvy about changes that are occurring in a rapidly evolving digital world than most adults are. So wouldn't it make sense to allow them a significant hand in designing curricula in their schools based on those changes—particularly now that the world of adult work is occurring increasingly online?

In addition, this sort of working partnership between teacher and student in which the two research together changes that are occurring in the world of adult work, and then work together to design a curriculum for the student, would not only involve young people more fully in their education, but would also directly connect them to the reasons why they would be learning specific subject matter.

Furthermore, if one looks carefully at a number of core standards that have been established for various subject matter by the Common Core Standards Initiative, and then looks at changes that are occurring in the world of professional expertise related to those same subject areas, it is easy to see certain disconnects that might be occurring between standards that Common Core has determined for various age groups of students in different subject areas and what is transpiring in various disciplines from the world of adult expertise that might be integrally related to those same subject matters. For instance, as was previously mentioned, those scientists now working at Harvard's Institute for Biologically Inspired Engineering, are focused more on processes that lead toward real-world solutions by taking what they have learned from various experiments and then tweaking that information across various disciplines, rather than dwelling only on conclusions they might have reached. This was certainly the case with chemist Joanna Aizenberg, who developed nonstick surfaces for such things as airplane wings by taking what she had learned by studying the surface of the insect-trapping pitcher plant and then utilizing a similar process in developing real-world applications.

In other words, as information and knowledge that at one time might have appeared final is so rapidly transformed in order to provide real-world solutions to various problems, and as scientists working in various disciplines are now able to communicate with each other more quickly than ever, the processes that lead toward various creative solutions in different areas are often seemingly becoming more important to engender than even final results.

Yet, if one looks at the Common Core science standards for grades six through twelve, one sees an almost exclusive emphasis on checking facts, determining results, or analyzing scientific and technical presentations, rather than on how young people might learn to use scientific processes across different disciplines to determine creative solutions to real-world problems. That is, nowhere is there any mention of students learning to apply results they have obtained from various experiments they have conducted to real-world situations in which they might be interested, as Ms. Aizenberg did. Nor is there seemingly any mention of students learning to conduct experiments that are similar to each other in different areas of endeavor.

Although, of course, learning how to employ the scientific method, how to conduct experiments, and how to draw inferences from various scientific writings are important skills for budding scientists to acquire, it would seem that if those skills are not carefully partnered with learning the creative process that is at the heart of scientific inquiry, then particularly in our current digital age, something significant is missing from the science education of those in their formative years.

Similarly, if one looks at the Common Core history/social studies standards for grades six through twelve, one finds certain important components relative to learning history and social studies in our modern world nearly entirely missing. That is, there is a heavy emphasis in the standards on such things as evaluating authors' differing points of view on the same historical event or issue, analyzing in detail a series of historical events described in a text, or identifying key steps in a text's description of a process related to history/social studies (e.g., how a bill becomes a law or how interest rates are raised or lowered).

However, at the same time, there appears to be little or no emphasis on skills that might engender more creative thinking, such as learning to integrate significant historical events with developments in other areas, such as that of scientific experimentation, or the study of geography related to various changing weather patterns; or learning to relate how governments operate to the behavior of certain individuals; or learning how culture might determine the history or politics of a particular country.

In other words, there is a heavy emphasis on the processes of analysis, identification, and logic, with seemingly little or no emphasis on how to integrate the various dynamic aspects that are part of a specific area of history or social studies into a coherent whole. And yes, it is important for students to learn how to effectively use logic and cogent analysis when learning either history or culture, yet it seems that if from the beginning they don't learn how to examine social and historical situations more creatively, they might lose the ability to do so when they inherit a world in which events surrounding them transpire at increasing rates of speed.

The Core Standards related to science, and to social studies and history, it would seem, are significant examples of why teachers and students working together to develop subject matter and curricula from what is transpiring in the world of adult work would tend to be a better way to connect learning to the world of adult expertise for which students are preparing. That is, the Core Standards often appear to emanate from entrenched preconceived ideas of what is important for young people to learn within different subject areas, rather than emanating from a dynamic view of the world of professional expertise outside the schoolhouse door as it relates to those same areas of learning.

IDEAS FOR REFLECTION

If a more dynamic, relevant approach to learning in which teacher and student work as equal partners to design curricula based on real-world occurrences is to indeed become a reality, the role of the teacher in the modern classroom is obviously going to have to change significantly. More than anything, it is going to have to embody those two principles that are to be found throughout the writings of John Dewey—reality of encounter and continuum of experience—two aspects of the teacher-student relationship that tend to be missing today in the vast majority of schools, even many of the more progressive ones.

In terms of the preceding discussion, this would mean that teachers would need to work with students as equal partners in examining how various subject matter might be derived from the world of adult expertise that teacher and student have researched together, with adults providing the proper amount of knowledge, expertise, and natural adult authority whenever necessary, yet also permitting students to take the lead whenever that seems appropriate, particularly in accessing various developments occurring in the digital world about which many young people tend to be more savvy.

It would also mean that the two of them would need to agree beforehand to take their investigations of the world of adult work outside of school just as far as they need to be taken for the purpose of deriving subject matter that is relevant and meaningful to the student, This means that those investigations wouldn't be subject to artificial constraints such as a predetermined curriculum that prepares students to achieve certain scores on standardized tests, or to a rigid daily schedule that wouldn't allow enough time for student and teacher to proceed with their research of recent occurrences within the world of adult work.

In addition, it would be important that teachers and students attempt to establish partnerships with working professionals in various fields of expertise, professionals who would be able to provide them with information concerning recent developments in those fields that might be applicable to the creation of various learning progressions. Hopefully, as such partnerships progressed, there would be an ongoing, immediate relationship established between cutting-edge events and changes in various fields of endeavor and subject matter that teacher and student create together by directly employing those events and changes.

In fact, it is difficult to see how students and teachers could work together to effectively create learning progressions for various subject areas based on occurrences in the world of adult work unless there is a consistent partnering with experts from the world of professional expertise who would be willing to share certain cutting-edge developments from their particular field of endeavor—those that teachers and students could then employ to create their

own subject matter and curricula. So this then is the subject of the chapter
that follows.

Chapter Seven

The World Outside of School

Except for the occasional field trip, learning in most elementary, middle, and secondary schools takes place almost exclusively inside the typical, self-contained classroom, where students are taught subject matter by a teacher who uses either what resources her school has provided her, or else employs her own creativity to design learning activities that she hopes will engage her students. Seldom does one hear of regular, ongoing connections between the students in a particular classroom and experts from the world of adult work. Yet, at the same time, it is this movement of academic learning into the world outside of school that might energize young people's creative impulses as effectively as anything that takes place within their classrooms themselves.

For reasons that seem rather obvious, visiting the laboratory of a working chemist, physicist, or medical researcher, the studio of an artist, a busy newspaper room, the offices of lawyers who are preparing cases or investors who are investing the money of their clients, or a store that specializes in creating and then selling something esoteric such as different types of oriental paper are activities that are certainly going to leave vivid impressions on many young people. These visits will also deepen students' level of general interest in specific subject matter that relates to what they have just apprehended in the world outside their classroom and school.

Every Friday at our school in Evanston, we attempted to find some place outside of school where we could take our students. These were places such as the former famous particle accelerator at Fermilab in the Chicago suburbs; the federal building downtown where we could observe trials involving law suits; the studios of recording engineers, architects, or artists working in anything from metal work to sculpture; newspaper rooms; various dramatic productions at professional theaters in the evenings; or even on one occasion, a visit to a local funeral parlor for those students who were brave enough to journey there. What we were never really able to accomplish, however, was to make significant connections between these journeys into the world outside of school and subject matter that students were attempting to absorb. What often occurred, unfortunately, was that after we took our students into the world of professional expertise, and they had become genuinely interested in what they had apprehended at a place of adult work or some other potentially interesting place in the community, we were not able to effectively develop curricula and learning progressions with our students that would allow them to follow through on their interests.

Occasionally, as in the case of the group of older students who were learning about the law, the court system, and the United States Constitution, and who went on to observe a number of civil and criminal trials, we were able to connect what young people had observed outside of school to their academic learning. However, unfortunately, what usually occurred after one of our Friday field trips, was that although the particulars of the trip might come up in discussion the following week with several of our students, still we had no genuine structure in place that would have allowed for the development of any meaningful learning progressions to evolve from any of these trips.

The reason why I mention this failure of our school to effectively follow through on journeys to places of adult work is to make a certain point: that if classroom structures are not in place to allow for ongoing connections between workplaces of professional expertise and the development of curricula by students and teacher working together to engender these, then a real opportunity to engender more creative thinking and learning in those young students will soon be lost. However, if lessons and learning progressions were created with the specific goal in mind of facilitating more creative approaches toward subject matter by building upon experiences that students may have had while connecting with the professional community outside of school, then it would seem that this might be one of the most effective ways to engender the very type of creative thinking that will be a key to students' future success in our current information age and digital world.

What is being proposed here is a model for connecting students to the world outside their classrooms, a world in which teachers would serve essentially as conduits in connecting their students to interesting, complex knowledge and information from the world of busy professionals who might be willing to work with them so that the students' curiosities could be engendered and their initiative as learners could be emboldened.

That is, by developing lessons that would allow their students to not only effectively absorb that to which they have been exposed by a particular expert, but also to prepare them for what they might come into contact with next in the lab, studio, or office to which they are journeying, teachers would be directly connecting, on a regular basis, meaningful learning in their classroom to the world that exists outside it so that their students might be able to imagine creative ways to absorb particular subject matter.

For example, a middle school teacher and a small group of students who are working together to create a biology curriculum based on cutting-edge developments in the world of medical research might partner with a researcher who is working with new techniques for accessing different gene maps associated with the sort of genetic fingerprinting currently being used to determine the guilt or innocence of criminals accused of various crimes. Or perhaps they might work with the most recent ways to study different cells that might be used for prenatal screening for certain potential diseases. In partnering with the medical researcher, the teacher and students would be able to develop a curriculum involving such things as how the process of heredity works, what the DNA molecule is and how it replicates itself, or what the different parts of the cell are—all based on their connection with cutting-edge developments that interest them in the world of medical research related to genetic fingerprinting or prenatal screening.

During the time they are connecting with the researcher, the students and teacher could also communicate regularly with him via e-mail, Facebook, Twitter, or text messaging as they work to develop their unique learning progressions involving biological science. For instance, they could send him various inheritance charts that they have created from the expertise that he has shared with them. Or perhaps they could even conduct their own mock investigations of a crime scene based on the information they have garnered from the researcher involving a hypothetical gene map as they work to develop an original curriculum of their own.

Employing much the same dynamic, another group of students could communicate with a university physicist, even on occasion visiting her lab, where she might teach them, for example, about the chemical properties of various laser beams, or even provide them with different versions of space-time diagrams, the schematic drawings that depict the collision of various high-speed subatomic particles. The students could then send the physicist charts or drawings they have created that demonstrate how different laser beams might be created from various chemicals, or space-time diagrams of their own that they have imagined from learning progressions that they have created with their teacher back at school regarding the behavior of various subatomic particles. In a manner similar to the sort of working relationship that might be developed with someone doing research in the biological sciences, this type of partnership with a working physicist would greatly facilitate students and teachers' working together to create unique, original learning progressions in the physical sciences.

Yet, at the same time, unless these connections between students and experts occur on a regular, rather than an intermittent basis, the sort of creative thinking that might be engendered in young people will have significantly less opportunity to grow fully to fruition. That is, it will tend to be swallowed by more narrowly conceived approaches to subject matter that many students now find occurring on a regular basis in their classrooms.

Therefore, there would seem to be two immediate tasks at hand in developing this new model for education in which local schools and the world of professional expertise might be seamlessly connected. One would obviously be to involve working professionals in the education of young people who are being schooled within their midst. The other would be to change the nature of teaching and learning in many classroom settings in order that this ongoing connection with the world of professional expertise might actually take place.

Needless to say, successful partnerships between students in their formative years in which teachers serve essentially as conduits whose duty it is to assist them in absorbing the complex information and knowledge to which they have been recently exposed in the world outside the schoolhouse door are going to require certain significant changes in how different areas of learning are presented to students. In particular, as was alluded to in earlier chapters, subject matter would need to be expanded to allow for the sort of creative thinking that might be engendered when students partner with professionals and experts, and so that young people might develop increased initiative to learn based on those partnerships; and also so that young people's impressions and curiosities might be more fully included in the development of various curricula and learning progressions that evolve directly from their connections to the world of the working professional.

Yet it is hard to see how this more expansive approach to subject matter might occur unless there is a certain amount of abdication of responsibilities by teachers in regard to the implementation of preconceived curricula put in place to either produce certain empirical test scores or to carefully follow a national core curricula—and at the same time, unless there is a concurrent acceptance of their increased responsibility for researching the advanced information and knowledge that is currently part of the world of professional expertise.

In fact, this type of research was exactly how I was able, in my own fumbling way, to create the physical science curriculum for the three twelve-year-old boys who learned theoretical physics with me. In addition to reading *A Brief History of Time*, I also read *The Tao of Physics* by Fritjof Capra, and in so doing, came upon the space-time diagrams that I recognized immediately would hold a genuine fascination for my three students, all of whom were highly artistically inclined. Because I wanted to know more about these representations of the subatomic world, and because I knew my three students would enjoy creating their own diagrams, we soon found ourselves further researching the subatomic world by studying the work of various theoretical physicists.

Once again, I soon came across Werner Heisenberg's uncertainty principle, which concerns the inability of physicists to observe a particle's position and velocity at the same time. Immediately recognizing that this idea would be extremely interesting to my students, because of its inherently peculiar, paradoxical nature in relation to what I knew about the students' unique, curious natures, I suggested we research how to make diagrams that depicted the idea more fully. As a result, the four of us soon found ourselves entering the domain of quantum physics, a world that, it would seem, due to its own tenuous nature, must almost necessarily be approached in the sort of indirect manner that rules out a more formal approach to teaching and learning— something that was in fact perfect for how our school actually operated.

In much the same way, while teaching a group of older students about the Bill of Rights in the United States Constitution, I spent time in one of the local libraries researching actual case law, scoured the local papers for stories that I thought might be turned into interesting legal cases if they ever came to trial, and even browsed the Internet to see if any constitutions of countries other than the United States might be available there. These things I did in lieu of simply using a typical middle-school text concerning the United States Constitution and its history.

Of course, the next step, that which is being proposed here as a means to more fully stimulate young people's inner worlds, would have been to arrange regular meetings with physicists working at Fermilab or the University of Chicago, and with local judges and attorneys. Although admittedly these connections did not occur at our school in the manner in which they might have, the point being made here is that if teachers of students in their formative years would rely less on traditional texts and preconceived curricula, and more on their investigations of subject areas that take place in the world of professional expertise, then the possibility of meaningful connections with experts from the domain of adult work could be significantly facilitated.

Obviously, these proposed connections between students, teachers, and working professionals have to begin somewhere. Possibly, they could be initiated by superintendents, principals, or teachers whose schools exist in large urban areas, where there would be any number of opportunities to connect with professionals in different fields of endeavor. These educators could get the proverbial ball rolling by approaching universities or hospitals engaged in specific types of research, different businesses, law firms, local banks and newspapers, computer programmers, or well-known artists, writers, or musicians living in a particular locale. Then, after these partnerships with those from the world of professional expertise were cultivated, teachers and students, working together, could begin developing innovative curricula and learning progressions that would allow the students to absorb, as fully as possible, the complex information, knowledge, and skills to which the working professional was exposing them.

For example, as a group of students was connecting with a geneticist or medical researcher who is looking for certain patterns that occur in the human genome, the students, along with their teacher, by using various charts or diagrams that the geneticist or researcher has provided them, could use some of the basic algebra that they had learned to look for similar patterns that might be occurring in someone's genetic makeup. Or, after connecting with a reporter at a local newspaper, the students and teachers could work together to develop a program for expository writing that employs not only the different methods that the reporter has shared with them for researching a story, but likewise the different techniques employed by various journalists or writers of nonfiction in producing their stories or books. Or a curriculum for learning mathematics might evolve from students and teachers working together to create their own simulated bank, with the assistance of a local banker; or developing their own abbreviated version of an investment portfolio, with the assistance of a stock analyst or investment banker. Needless to say, there would be many important mathematical skills addressed in these endeavors, from the basic idea of a ratio or function, to how to apprehend important patterns in a group of figures, to algebraic thought itself.

While these partnerships were being developed in large urban areas, where connections between local schools and experts working in a specific field would be easier to facilitate simply because of the number of working professionals in a particular geographic area, perhaps an actual national directory of professionals who would be willing to make themselves available to students could be created. This could be done largely through e-mail, text messaging, Facebook, Twitter, or YouTube, which would obviously allow students and experts to connect with each other from a distance.

Obviously, creating these partnerships among young people and working professionals is going to take a certain amount of organization and willpower. Yet, again, if school boards, administrators, and classroom teachers would be willing to let go of certain aspects of their occupations to which they now devote so much time and energy—such as time spent preparing students for higher scores on standardized tests by focusing on only certain parts of a particular curriculum—in lieu of taking on the new responsibility of serving as conduits between young people and the world of professional expertise, then the collective will to accomplish this might indeed be summoned.

Particularly in our current digital age, the type of creative learning that will better prepare students for the world they will soon inherit exists increasingly in the world of professional expertise outside of school, rather than exclusively in the modern classroom. Therefore, one of the most important challenges of modern education will be how to effectively integrate those two worlds so that the scope of subject matter begins to expand beyond what it is by merging with the primary reason why most subject matter exists—

that is, to give young people the skills and knowledge they will need in order to be successful in the world they are about to inherit.

In 2011, with the goal in mind of creating long-term partnerships with those from the world of professional expertise that are meaningful for students and also sustainable for those employers who are partnering with the students, and that would transform the depth of learning in science, technology, engineering, and math, the Opportunity Equation, along with the Carnegie Corporation of New York, launched an online competition involving colleges and professional organizations aimed at identifying and encouraging ideas that lead toward the development of such long-term partnerships between students and experts in various fields. Along with its report of the competition, the Opportunity Equation issued a statement concerning the need to educate students at increasingly higher levels in STEM (science, technology, engineering, math) fields of endeavor, likewise referring to the fact that despite the best efforts of our nation's teachers and principals, many of our schools are ill-equipped to do just that—despite the reality that our communities are filled with the world's best professionals in many different fields.

As a result, Opportunity Equation asked the question: What if schools of higher learning and institutions that are involved in one of the STEM fields worked to connect the world of professional expertise with teachers and students in meaningful, lasting ways that most existing partnerships between students and professional experts—because of their short-term nature—are unable to achieve?

The operative word is obviously long-term. That is, while one hears constantly of schools becoming involved with those from the world of adult work in order to provide short-term programs, demonstrations, field trips, or even visits to the school by an expert, one tends to seldom hear of the sort of long-term associations with working professionals in which information, knowledge, and skills flow back and forth on a steady basis, with classroom teachers serving as regular conduits between students and working professionals.

In addition, as Allison Craiglow Hockenberry wrote in her 2011 essay in the *Huffington Post,* "In Our New Sputnik Moment, the Solutions are Down on the Ground," while many institutions already support schools with various programs—museums and local colleges being significant examples—there are many other people and organizations that one would not initially think of as partners for lasting change within our schools. To this end, some of the organizations that Hockenberry mentions in her piece are architectural firms, graphic designers, construction companies, urban planners, electrical engineers, environmental waste managers, bankers, and software engineers. She likewise goes on to suggest that various professionals in these fields could not only introduce students in their formative years to careers they may never have heard or dreamed of, but in addition show them specifically what they need to learn in order to become successful in those careers. Consequently, programs such as this would be a step even further down the road from merely developing learning progressions and subject matter from developments within the world of professional expertise.

In order to implement them, schools and classroom teachers could actually work with students to create curricula directly from what they have learned from experts in their field about the important skills and knowledge necessary to succeed in a particular career, thus directly relating classroom learning at a whole new level to the preparation necessary to succeed in our current information age and digital world. Obviously, such a direct connection between career paths in various fields and what young people need to learn to be successful in those careers is now missing from the vast majority of our schools, as is the opportunity for students to have a direct hand in developing subject matter (of course with the assistance of their teachers) that they imagine will prepare them for the life they might wish to pursue as adults. By directly connecting those two things, schools would be able to achieve a degree of relevancy in their purpose that not even visionary pioneers such as John Dewey could have imagined decades ago.

In addition, websites could be developed that would allow students to communicate with professionals willing to participate on an ongoing, regular basis. For example, the names, e-mail addresses, a brief description of their field of expertise and what they are currently working on, as well as specific times of availability for the various experts could be placed on the site. Then, students in classrooms throughout the country, or the world for that matter, would have the opportunity to ask those experts questions or seek clarification regarding different areas of learning for which they are endeavoring to develop learning progressions or subject matter with the assistance of their teachers.

Furthermore, if students were able to connect in such a manner with experts in various fields of endeavor, those students would gain powerful allies in developing their own learning progressions. For with continuous advice and direction coming from those who are professionally aware of how various subject matter that young people learn in school might be connected to a particular area of expertise, the field of information and knowledge with which students are engaged would inevitably grow significantly larger. Hence, there would be many more opportunities for truly creative learning to take place as students use this expanded field to create their own approaches to different areas of learning.

In other words, if some type of nationally organized mentoring program could be created in which experts in various fields of endeavor agreed to make themselves available to students through regular connections on the

Web, boundaries for different subject areas, particularly the sciences, could be expanded exponentially.

One tends to hear over and over today how this country's young people are not turned on by science. And educators and parents wonder how we can make science more interesting to our students so that they might be prepared to compete with students in India, China, or Japan in the global economy. As one hears this concern, one has to sometimes wonder exactly what the difficulty is. For many of the great scientists—Einstein, Newton, Darwin—approached their important discoveries with an extraordinary amount of intuitive thinking, almost as curious children would. For instance, Newton experimented with placing his prisms in a certain relational order and then discovered that white light is actually composed of all the different colors of the spectrum, rather than being changed into these different colors by the prism itself. Einstein, gazing at the clock tower in Bern, suddenly realized the extraordinary implications for long-held ideas about space and time that the invariant speed of light represented. Or James Watson and Francis Crick worked feverishly to build their tinker toy–like model of the chemical structure of DNA on their way to realizing that its chemical structure is in fact a double-helix that wraps itself around the outside, not the inside, of a sugar-phosphate backbone.

Once again, if one looks at how Jean Piaget and other cognitive psychologists have observed the investigations by a child of his world, and then compares the dynamics that are a part of these to what occurs inside the minds of great scientists or thinkers doing important work, it is entirely possible that one might find certain significant characteristics that the two voyages of discovery have in common. For example, Howard Gardner, in his book *Creating Minds*, which explains how the creativity exemplified by great minds such as Einstein, Freud, Picasso, or Stravinsky might have evolved, refers to the research of historian Isaiah Berlin to explain how Einstein's genius had very much to do with being able to conceive of what cannot in principle be imagined or expressed in ordinary language. That is, Einstein was able to sustain, beyond the realm of language, a vision of a unified, harmonious, physically caused world.

Likewise, Piaget, in discussing how ideas form in children, refers to the notion that when a child constructs a particular idea to correspond to the world of adult language, the idea may originally be entirely the child's, in the sense that the words that express it are initially as hazy to his intelligence as a certain physical phenomena might be; and so to understand it, he has to deform and then assimilate it according to mental structures that he himself has created. In addition, if one looks at these two worlds more closely, it becomes rather obvious that neither the child discovering his immediate environment nor an adult discoverer uncovering some new piece of the universe could proceed optimally with their investigations unless their inner worlds had already become energized. In fact, in the case of someone like Einstein, it was the actual strength of his impressions and curiosities that fueled the highly intuitive approach that he employed to investigate time and space in his entirely unique manner.

So the problem with how science is now taught in many schools might have to do with how it is not presented to students in their formative years by actual scientists, who embody this same intuitive, fully energized approach to scientific investigation. Instead, science is usually taught to students by professional educators who tend to present it as either empirical knowledge that the students are required to learn, or even worse, in terms of a specific educational method—as one can certainly see as one scans the rigid requirements of the current Common Core Standards in science for students in grades six through twelve.

For it would seem that nothing kills interest in young people in a specific subject matter, particularly scientific investigation of one's world, more than turning it into a rigidly preconceived learning sequence with specific endpoints that are subject to adult evaluation and judgment.

IDEAS FOR REFLECTION

If a more seamless approach to educating students in their formative years, one in which they are fully connected to the world of professional expertise, is going to be adopted in our schools, then it would seem that educators are going to have to take a more expansive view of their job description. In short they are going to need to realize more fully than they do now that the lives and learning of their students, the environment in which they are educated, and the world outside the classroom door are all one.

For although schooling obviously has a very important function to fulfill in our society, if the school environment is kept separate from the world of adult work, the larger society in which students live, and particularly the world of professional expertise, then young people's learning will inevitably become stifled. Hence, it will not be the sort of creative learning that will optimally prepare them for the global marketplace and information age that they will soon be entering.

With this in mind, it would seem more important than ever that the traditional boundaries for schooling begin to burst open in the same manner in which the World Wide Web has burst open the boundaries in the worlds of business, technology, science, and the arts. For to continue with the idea that schooling is something that largely takes place within self-contained classrooms is to in fact restrain the sort of creative approaches that students will need to develop in order to be successful in the world they are about to inherit.

Yet this endeavor is simply not going to come into existence as fully as it might if educators are not willing to give up a certain measure of control over the academic learning of their students. In short, they are going to have to come to the realization that one of the best ways that young people can be prepared for participation in today's global marketplace is by being given a greater hand in creating their own subject matter based on developments in the world of adult work that are occurring outside the classroom door.

However, there is one specific danger that might potentially arise in terms of this effort to connect students more fully to the world of professional expertise. If the World Wide Web were to become the primary, even exclusive, means by which those in their formative years connect themselves to the adult world outside of school, then it appears rather easy to see how those connections, because they often tend to involve only young people's cognitive lives and their basic computer skills, might become just as limiting as those rigidly preconceived classroom activities that can so easily dull the potential richness of students' developing inner lives.

This issue of how young people connecting with others around a particular subject area exclusively through the Internet could have a potentially deleterious effect on their inner lives is one that is admittedly complex. As much as anything, it would appear to involve a discussion of the nature of the relationship that is engendered with a specific area of one's world when that association is largely virtual. Therefore, this topic will be dealt with in more detail within the chapter that follows.

Chapter Eight

The Inner Lives of Children in the Digital Age

Thirty years ago, the late, great media critic Neil Postman wrote of how, with the emergence of television into our lives during the middle of the twentieth century, childhood was not left fully intact due to the ever-greater intrusion of many of the particulars of adult life into the television programs that children watched. That is, many aspects of the adult world that had been previously kept away from children until they were more ready to absorb them began seeping into their lives. In doing so, Postman contended, children were not given a similar amount of time to fully inhabit the childhood that previous generations had enjoyed.

Now, of course, with the advent of the Internet, the world of childhood is once again being impacted in a dramatic way. Only this time, it would seem, it is not so much the difference in the content of what children are being exposed to that might be affecting them in powerful ways. It is the actual mode in which information and knowledge arrives on their computer screen or other digital devices that is so fundamentally different from what they might experience in the world of real-life situations and people.

Therefore, what might need to be studied, particularly in terms of how young people can learn more creatively in preparation for the information age that they will soon enter, is the potential relationship that might exist between virtual learning and the growth of curiosity and creative instincts within young people whose emotive lives are yet evolving. In short, the question that seemingly needs to be asked is: Do curiosities, natural interests, and rich impressions develop in the same manner inside children while they are learning if their access to various subject matter takes place largely online in a virtual world, as opposed to the world of living, breathing people and real-world situations? More specifically, is the difference between these two modes of learning profound enough that it in fact changes the actual nature of the relationship between a student and what he learns?

When a group of students at our school were learning about viruses, proteins, genetic material, and other such microorganisms, they were able to use complex schematic, three-dimensional models, which the biochemistry department of a certain university had included on their website, to accurately construct their own models of these organisms out of all manner of materials that we found in the art cabinet of our school, and also at the local arts and crafts store in downtown Evanston.

Previously, before the Internet and Web became an important part of all our lives in the early and mid-1990s, it would have been extremely difficult for me, as these students' teacher, to not only track down the complex models of microorganisms that I was able to access online, many of them almost certainly created from pictures that had been taken by the type of high-powered microscopes that are found only in the sophisticated labs to which this particular university had direct access. It would likewise have been just as improbable that I would have been able to gain immediate access to the advanced information and knowledge that was similarly posted on their website in conjunction with these three-dimensional models.

In this particular case, and in many others like it, because I had, as a teacher of students in their formative years, this immediate access to complex information and knowledge online, and because I could then immediately develop lessons that employed it, the pace at which our students were able to learn various subject matter was expanded exponentially from what it had been previously, before the advent of the current digital age.

Therefore, the capacity that teachers now have to not only develop lessons for their students that employ the use of highly complex information and knowledge that beforehand would probably have never found its way into the typical elementary or middle school classroom, but also to direct their students to this same advanced material, is obviously the sort of significant development that tends to permanently change both teaching and learning. So, in this respect, the introduction of the Internet and Web into the world of education and learning has been nothing but positive.

At the same time, however, there appears to be a certain danger presented by information and knowledge garnered by young people that is largely virtual. This is simply that such access might remain exclusively cognitive and perceptual in nature, meaning that young people may be accessing it only with a certain limited part of themselves. In other words, the question becomes one of examining how energized the particulars of students' inner lives, those dynamics that have been examined earlier in this work, will become if the objects of their learning remain only those virtual ones that appear in front of them on the screen of their computer.

John Taylor Gatto, in his classic book, *Dumbing Us Down*, has written of how networks don't require the participation of the whole person, but only a narrow piece, meaning that all those parts of oneself that don't involve what he calls the *network-interest part*, tend to be suppressed. Although Gatto was writing about this concern in the early 1990s, and so was referring not to the Internet, but to the basic function of networking that traditional schooling tends to serve, his point would appear to be even more relevant to our current computer-driven age, which obviously represents the process of networking in one of its purest, most direct forms.

For as young people sit at their computers, accessing even the sort of previously inaccessible complex information that we used at our school to teach our students microbiology, one wonders what the possible repercussions are for their emotive lives if the particular subject area that they are learning remains entirely virtual. That is, if they become highly dependent upon the World Wide Web to provide them with information and knowledge from a particular subject area, rather than also be given a significant amount of assistance by their teachers in how to relate this knowledge and information to the larger community of people and real-world objects to which they might have access, will this development tend to produce dulled, disembodied experience within them? That is, will their curiosities and interests be fully stimulated, and will their impressions be able to grow to fruition if the academic subject matter with which they come into contact occurs largely in the virtual world of their computer screen? Or conversely, for these sort of inner dynamics to become fully realized, do children's inner lives necessarily need to come into consistent contact with real-world learning situations, and real people teaching and guiding them while they learn?

Hubert L. Dreyfus, professor of philosophy at the University of California at Berkeley, and oftentimes critic of artificial intelligence, makes the point in his book *On the Internet (Thinking in Action)* that as we learn, our physical body is involved in that learning in a number of ways. These are: our ability to move around in the world, our moods that make things matter to us, our location within a particular context in which we have to cope with things and other people, and the ways in which we are exposed to disappointment and failure.

Dr. Dreyfus goes on to say that as we advance through different stages of learning, we become increasingly dependent upon our embodied nature, meaning that the further we advance, the more we must directly, and not remotely, be involved with the actual task environment itself while dealing with both people and things. Consequently, according to Dreyfus, the supposed richness and opportunities of the Internet can often prove illusory simply because they do not include this embodied self.

Within the same context, Rosemary Lehman, a specialist in distance education at the University of Wisconsin in Madison, points out in a 2006 article on creating instructor and learner presence in the distance education experience that research in the fields of both neurobiology and psychology that looks at the effect of human emotions on brain function is beginning to reveal that there is in fact a critical relationship between behavior, cognition, and emotion—hence the need to view them as integrated, rather than as separate components of each other.

What the writings and research of Dr. Dreyfus, Dr. Lehman, and others argue for of course is a consideration of mind, body, and emotions in relation to one another as a means to facilitate more effective and creative learning, particularly in light of our current digital age. So, taking this into consideration, the question once again becomes: What effect might digital learning have on the depth and intensity with which young learners are able to experience their curiosities, interests, and impressions? Even more to the point, which aspects of a child's inner life that have to do with him developing a creative mind-set are being optimally stimulated when he or she is learning a particular subject matter solely by accessing the relevant information and knowledge online? And which parts of that more emotive world have little or no relationship to what he is apprehending on his computer screen?

In order to answer these questions, it would appear to be necessary to examine two different aspects of the child's inner life in relation to how they might tend to evolve in the virtual world. These would be the development of natural interests and curiosities, and the germination of strongly experienced impressions.

As anyone who has spent much time around children is already aware, curiosity in those who are still in their formative years is very much an organic force that tends to move quickly from one object in the child's environment to the next. That is, it is something fluid that, if it is to be kept alive and nurtured, must be allowed its inevitable forward movement. Otherwise it begins to stultify and die. In fact, often one of the most difficult challenges of teaching children is how to properly direct their innate curiosity about a particular learning area without killing it by too severely limiting it.

Of course, those proponents of online learning who might be reading this are almost certainly thinking that this is one of the real values of accessing various subject matter online; the opportunity that young learners might have to move seamlessly from certain information to other information with just a click of their mouse. However, as is often true when looking at the dynamics of children's inner lives, all is not what it might seem.

For just as preconceived lessons that do not include input from students prior to their implementation tend to constrict a child's curious impulses, so preprogrammed learning that takes place solely inside the parameters of a computer screen often tends to produce the same negative result for two significant reasons. One is that online programs, because they are usually designed by someone who does not personally know the children who use them, and who is not part of their learning environment, cannot possibly be inclusive of spontaneous interests and curiosities that might arise in the children who learn by using these programs.

The other reason is simply that such learning is in fact taking place only inside the parameters of one's computer screen, rather than within the larger environment of interpersonal relations, and real-life objects and situations. This means that the overall field in which the fluid nature of childhood curiosity might evolve is being limited simply because the child's attention is being so acutely focused on the screen in front of him. As a result, his curiosity is not being given the sort of free rein that it might otherwise have within the context of a much larger milieu.

There is also the question of how fully various impressions are being allowed to germinate inside young people when their learning of a certain subject is taking place largely online. That is, is there an actual difference between the strength of impressions that virtual images might engender in them, and the intensity that corresponding real-world experiences and objects might bring about?

For example, a group of children are looking at slides of various microorganisms under a microscope. In doing so, they become fascinated by the almost malignant, otherworldly nature of these strange creatures that they are apprehending—to the point where those impressions grow inside them with a certain potency. Now, if those children were to look at virtual images of the same microorganisms on a particular website, would the impressions growing inside them reach a similar level of intensity? That, it would seem, is really the question when it comes to the effect that our current digital age may be having on the strength of young people's impressions, and also on the development of their curiosities and creative instincts. For if it is actually the case that virtual images accessed on one's computer engender impressions with significantly less potency than corresponding objects and situations found in the real world, then it would be important for educators to carefully examine how virtual learning might become fully integrated with real-life learning so that dulled inner experience is not consequently facilitated.

This is not an issue that is on many people's radar screens these days compared to questions concerning how effective preprogrammed online learning programs might be in producing significant academic learning in various subject areas. Yet ultimately it has enormous implications for how today's children might learn to learn more creatively so that their inner lives become energized, rather than dulled.

At the same time, because it is hard to provide any sort of statistical evidence for children's curiosities and impressions becoming diluted over time, this is a process that can go on entirely unexamined while a number of children grow toward adulthood with their inner experience being dulled by learning that is too-centered on the virtual world inside their computer.

Jean Piaget wrote of how children develop their intelligence through a process of assimilating new concepts into previously formed cognitive structures. Yet he also pointed out that this process tends to not take place as fully as it might if there is not a strong affective power drawing a child toward those parts of his immediate environment that he is attempting to apprehend. This means that if the objects and experiences with which a child is coming into contact are not affecting him as intensely as they otherwise might, the growth of the child's intelligence itself might be in danger of being diluted.

Therefore, it seems entirely possible to suggest that if virtual images on a digital screen do not affect children as impressionistically as their real-world counterparts might, it may not just be their emotive lives that are being compromised, but the growth of their creative intelligence as well—a growth that might become stifled by the amount of time that the children spend in the virtual world. For instance, if a child is making a connection online with something that might further his ability to form concrete concepts and to think logically, and that virtual connection does not occur within him with as much intensity as its counterpart in the real world does, then it seems possible to suggest that both the strength of any concepts that he might be assimilating, as well as the power of his actual reasoning in relation to them, might be evolving within him in a duller, more diluted manner.

Yes, of course, activities such as learning mathematics are most likely going to affect young learners with a similar or even greater degree of intensity if they take place in the digital world rather than through the world of books, paper, and pencil. Yet there may be many other aspects of a child's cognitive development that, if apprehended primarily virtually, might not develop with a similar degree of intensity as they otherwise might, two of these being his apprehension of the physical and biological worlds.

For instance, if a child's introduction to the biological world of unseen plant or animal life occurs primarily through static virtual images on his computer screen, rather than by actually looking at these through a microscope in his classroom or home, it seems entirely possible that his conceptions of the organic world of the unseen might not evolve within him to a point of full power or clarity. In similar fashion, if a child is introduced to the force of gravity or the phenomenon of light primarily digitally, rather than learning how they originate in the real world, he may be likewise developing a false conception of the actual power and beauty of those forces—a conception that, it would seem, can then easily become part of an incomplete cognitive development.

When various aspects of a child's world leave a strong impression upon him, he naturally grows more curious about them; and as he becomes more curious he wants to explore and discover more. Hence, as he explores and discovers more, assimilating more information about his world while doing so, new cognitive structures, and likewise previously existing ones, become inevitably strengthened. So, once again, if young people living in our current digital age are going to explore their world in the type of manner that optimally strengthens their cognitive capacities in relation to their creative lives, the issue of what effect a virtual image on a computer screen has upon a child's emotive life compared to what he might experience in the world of other people and real-life situation would seem to be one that needs to be carefully examined.

Nancy Carlsson-Paige, professor of education at Lesley University in Cambridge, Massachusetts, writes in her book *Taking Back Childhood* of how symbols that children apprehend on a digital screen don't provide as full an experience for them as interactions that they might have with real-world people and things. Then going on to say how playing games with apps is limited to what happens between the child and a device because it doesn't involve the child's body, brain, and senses, she likewise mentions how when a child plays computer games, he plays according to someone else's rules and design—something that is profoundly different from a child having an original idea to make or do something. Therefore, if one accepts this particular line of reasoning, one has to indeed ask if young people spending time sitting at their computer or staring into the plastic face of a smart phone might be affecting not only their cognitive intelligence, but likewise their capacity to be more creative in preparation for the world they will soon inherit.

Piaget himself writes of how during the period of concrete operations, which begins in a child around the age of seven or eight, the child's universe no longer consists primarily of objects (or of persons as objects) as it did during the previous sensorimotor period, but now also contains real-life people as subjects who have their own views of different situations that the child must necessarily reconcile with his own. In other words, if the child's intelligence is to develop properly by becoming less centered on self (in the cognitive sense of the word), his mental operations must necessarily involve not only a physical universe, but an interpersonal or social one as well.

Extrapolating from these ideas of Piaget's theory of childhood intelligence and those of Nancy Carlsson-Paige and others who are questioning the effects that our current digital world might be having on children's creative thinking and cognitive development, it would seem one might easily begin to question the practice of continually exposing young people in their formative years to virtual images on a computer screen that remain separate from the interpersonal world that Piaget claims is necessary for a complete cognitive development simply because it allows for the subjective views of others.

In their 2001 study concerning the advantages and drawbacks of online learning, researchers L. S. Cifuentes and Doris Yu-Chih point out how dependence on an unresponsive partner (i.e., one's computer) can often inevitably cause frustration in a learner, leading to a sense of detachment. This of course is precisely how a young person's inner experience can become dulled while learning. That is, he begins to detach himself, either knowingly or unknowingly, from whomever or whatever is providing him with information and knowledge to the point where he begins to significantly withdraw from the specific learning situation in which he finds himself. This is something that it seems would almost certainly not occur with the same degree of regularity if he were learning within an interpersonal, social environment that included other students his age and real-life teachers as it would if he were sitting immobile at a computer screen.

Ironically, it would seem, the very digital world that is bringing so much creativity and collaboration into the modern world of adult work, as well as having the potential to do so within classroom environments for those in their formative years, might also, at the same time, be adversely affecting the growth of young people's creative intelligence as they learn, simply because it does not fully provide them with those real-world connections that they very much need at a young age if both their cognitive development and creative instincts are to in fact proceed in a truly healthy manner.

Quite simply, virtual images on a computer will never be able to affect children with the same level of intensity as real-world experiences do simply because the isolating experience of staring into a computer screen while learning, even as one does so in conjunction with others, can never be the same as engaging with other people purely and directly in the real world. In fact, there has been research demonstrating that students who learn solely through computer assisted instruction, without the opportunity to give active responses in attempting to assimilate what they are endeavoring to learn, will not even learn as well.

In one such 2005 study conducted by Annamaria Jerome and Patricia M. Barbetta, two educational researchers from Florida International University College of Education, the researchers studied the difference, for a group of fifth grade students with learning disabilities who were learning social studies, between computer-assisted instruction that involved active student responses while interacting with real-life people and situations (i.e., responding verbally to a question, writing a sentence, reading out loud, etc.) and responses that did not. Their results showed that when the students were actively involved in other real-world activities while they learned while using a computer, they learned more effectively than when they did not.

In addition, one area of children's mental lives that is a key to their becoming creative learners, that of developing the increased capacity for abstract thought, might also be compromised by too much time spent in the virtual world.

In a 2009 article, "Principles and Practices Report on Online Enrichment and Extension for the Gifted and Talented," social science researchers Yong Wu and Zhicheng Ma, in discussing cognitive characteristics of gifted children, write of how gifted children have a greater ability for abstract thinking, which distinguishes them from other children. That is, parents and teachers have noticed that children with gifted potential are usually skilled in manipulating language or numbers, while also exhibiting the ability to handle abstract ideas. Therefore, what they need if their cognitive development is to reach its full potential is to be guided in how to take integrated subjects and abstraction work to an increasingly higher level.

At the same time, various writers and researchers, such as Daniel Pink, author of the 2005 book *A Whole New Mind: Moving from the Information Age to the Conceptual Age*, have written of how abstract thinking leads toward greater creativity, and of how if we want to be more innovative, we need to become more abstract. Yet, at the same time, according to Pink, people often tend to do the opposite of that which will allow them to think more abstractly and thus more creatively. That is, they intensify their focus on what they are apprehending rather than widen their view, thus drawing closer rather than stepping back.

The effect that this might have on abstract, creative thinking is dealt with in a 2009 article in *Scientific American*, "An Easy Way to Increase Creativity." Referring to a paper by researcher Lile Jia and two of her colleagues from the Department of Psychological and Brain Sciences at Indiana University, "Lessons from a Faraway Land: The Effect of Spatial Distance on Creative Cognition," the article points out that behavioral scientists who study such matters have demonstrated that increasing psychological distance so that a problem feels further away can actually increase creativity. That is to say, psychological distance affects the way we mentally represent things, so that distant things are represented in a relatively abstract way, while psychologically near things tend to seem more concrete. To this end, the article uses the example of a corn plant, in which a concrete representation would refer to the shape, color, taste, and smell of the plant, while connecting the item to its most common use—a food product. On the other hand, an abstract representation might refer to the corn plant as a source of energy or as a fast growing plant, with these more abstract thoughts then leading toward people's contemplating less common uses for corn, such as a source of ethanol, or using the plant to create mazes for children.

The point is that abstract thinking can make it easier for people to form surprising connections between seemingly unrelated concepts; something that has been discussed earlier in this work as being an important ingredient for young people learning to think more creatively in preparation for the information age they will soon inherit.

Therefore, when the idea that psychological distance from whatever subject area one is apprehending can increase one's abstract, creative thinking in relation to it is juxtaposed against the preconceived, step-by-step nature of most online learning, it seems easy to see how one might come to the conclusion that online learning has the potential to dull a young person's capacity for creative thought simply because, as he narrows his focus while following a series of predetermined steps on his computer screen, there tends to be increasingly less perspective, and thus less psychological distance between him and whatever he is endeavoring to assimilate. Hence, there is less opportunity for him to perceive whatever he is learning more abstractly and thus more creatively, as he would if he were holding it at arm's length, so to speak.

The development of a highly evolved, creative intelligence in young people, one that will become increasingly important to them as they prepare to enter our current information age, would appear to be integrally tied to both how strongly their emotive, inner lives grow energized as they learn, and how fully they are able to develop their capacity for abstract thought so that they can view different areas of learning with more perspective.

Therefore, if one accepts the idea that excess exposure to online learning, and to the digital world itself, can in fact negatively impact each of these dynamics, then once again, there would appear to be a genuine irony at the heart of how our digital age may be affecting those in their formative years. This is simply that although our present Internet-driven world makes it ever more important that one think expansively and creatively if one is to become successful, at the same time, the constant exposure to digital devices by young people may be in fact dulling a certain measure of that same creative intelligence.

Yet there must certainly be methods and learning environments for young people that, at one and the same time, use digital technology to stimulate young people's curiosities and impressions in conjunction with real-world experiences, while also providing them with enough psychological distance from whatever subject they are learning in order that they optimally develop the capacity for abstract thought, and thus their creativity. Project-based learning that employs various digital technologies, particularly when it is fused with the sort of real-world connections with experts from various areas of adult work alluded to in the previous chapter, might be one way to introduce Internet-based learning into children's lives in a manner in which neither the richness of their impressions and curiosities nor their capacity for abstract thought and creative intelligence is dulled by too much time spent in front of a computer screen.

In their 2007 book, *Reinventing Project-Based Learning: Your Field Guide to Real-World Projects in the Digital Age*, Suzie Boss, founding member of the Learning Innovation and Technology Consortium, and former classroom teacher Jane Krauss discuss their own evolution as educators toward the use of digital technologies in order to navigate new ways for students and teachers to work together in a project-based setting. Using as an example the evolution of high school humanities teacher Adam Kinroy, they explain how he moved from merely incorporating Internet-based technologies that were already in existence to classroom structures that use multimedia digital devices as the actual centerpieces of a new learning environment. His work included teaching students such skills as how to embed digitized film clips into their writing, thereby including actual visual imagery within a written piece, or teaching his students about different points of view in a short story by streaming audio clips from National Public Radio shows as a means of motivating them to develop their own podcasts.

Boss and Krauss go on to explain how educators around the world are using similar technologies to reinvent projects that are more inherently connected to students' own lives by moving away from traditional teaching toward a new vision of instructional design that seeks to include emerging technologies directly into learning in which students become more active participants than they had previously been. By expanding subject areas in such a way by directly connecting students with real-world media experiences, and by stimulating students to become more active participants in their learning, this sort of digitally driven, project-based learning encourages students to become both more expansive in their thinking and more collaborative with each other as they learn. Even more importantly though, is that such learning, although making full use of the latest digital devices, would seem to be centered on students using the latest technologies to further their own creative thinking, rather than instead being used by the technologies while they sit immobile at a computer screen.

However, there would still appear to be a certain dynamic that might potentially become a significant danger to this sort of creative, project-based learning. That is, if teachers and schools are under pressure to produce certain test scores related to areas of learning into which students are creatively incorporating their digitally-based projects, or if certain state or national core standards have a hand in determining the genesis of the projects themselves.

A recent article on the Web concerned a public high school in Austin, Texas devoted to teaching every subject to every student through the sort of project-based learning that includes a significant digital basis. To this end, the article and corresponding video on Edutopia's Twitter page involving their Schools That Work series demonstrated the resultant positive feedback by both students and teachers in the school who were permitted to teach and learn in such a manner. Yet it was also clear that much of the creative, project-based learning was put in place primarily so that students in the school could meet previously established state standards in various subject areas. That is, prior to the students developing projects using their digital devices related to their reading of the best-selling book *The Hunger Games*, their teacher outlined for them in advance certain state standards in both world history and English literature that students needed to absorb as they moved ahead with their projects.

For world history, there were such things as understanding the causes and impact of World War II or describing the emergence and characteristics of totalitarianism; while for English literature, the standards involved the development of such skills as the ability to analyze various scenes or different characters' moral dilemmas. In other words, the state standards were seemingly given to students in advance as things that they necessarily needed to incorporate into the body of their projects. To this end, the principal of the school even mentioned on the video that accompanied the article on Edutopia's site, "We have no choice what we teach. The state tells us what we have to teach."

This would seem to be an example of how test scores and national or state core standards might potentially have a significant negative effect on the type of project-based learning in which students can use the latest digital devices in order to learn more creatively in preparation for the world they are about to inherit. For if students are forced to limit the scope of their projects simply because what they are developing must originate with the need to meet certain core standards, it seems almost certain that their projects will soon become far less creative and unique in their scope than they otherwise might be. As a result, so will the thinking and learning of the students who create them.

As any good teacher knows, what occurs at the beginning of a lesson is what usually ends up determining both the scope and content of the lesson itself. So if the scope of students' projects—particularly those in which they employ the latest digital technologies—is necessarily limited at its inception by standards for learning to which the students are required to adapt themselves, those students' creativity will likewise be significantly limited by parameters that are inherently too narrow; just as subject matter in many of today's classrooms is being narrowed by the need for classroom teachers and principals to produce certain scores on standardized tests.

Ultimately, it would seem, a choice has to be made. Do we want to facilitate the sort of creative, collaborative thinking in young people that will serve them well in the current information age into which they are soon headed? Or do we accept the possibility of restricting that creative thinking by subjecting them to standards for learning that we as adults have determined in advance are necessary for success, even though some of the skills and knowledge to which those standards point are in fact remnants of an earlier age?

In terms of the possibility of engendering creativity and collaboration with others through project-based learning that employs the latest digital technologies, it would seem that to narrow and constrict these activities because of standards for learning that might be no longer applicable in a few years seems silly at best. At worst, it seems downright unfair to those young people whose creative lives might be adversely affected.

IDEAS FOR REFLECTION

Once again, due to how we now have become so connected with one another in our current digital age, and because of how information and knowledge now change so quickly, students in their formative years are going to need to increasingly develop both their capacity to imagine areas of learning more expansively and to collaborate with others while doing so. Yet, at the same time, there would appear to be a certain ironic danger lying at the heart of this same digital age—that both online learning progressions and a steady stream of virtual images on a computer screen, when disconnected from real-world experience, objects, and other people, might stifle the same creative instincts of young people that are going to become so necessary for their success in the current information age.

Therefore, it is going to become highly important, particularly as digital technologies become ever more prevalent and more complex in our modern world, that current approaches to classroom learning factor in the significance of students' acquiring various skills in ways that will allow them to use the technologies to expand their creative approaches to different subject matter, but to do so in a manner in which the technologies don't begin to use the students. As much as anything, it also would seem highly important that educators keep in mind the rather obvious yet easily forgotten fact that learning in the virtual world and learning that takes place in the world of other people, situations, and objects are two very different realities.

Naturally, as young students connect with others on the Web while developing a more expansive view of various subject matters, or develop projects that employ the latest digital devices, there is a genuine opportunity for more creative learning. Yet it would seem that if that enhanced creativity begins to take place exclusively in the virtual world, the same curiosities, impressions, and enriched inner life that are at the heart of all creative thought may become dangerously compromised in the bargain.

Chapter Nine

A Distracted Awareness and Creativity

Since the inception of our current digital age, a number of books and articles have been written about the effects that digital devices may be having on our attention spans and ability to concentrate, very likely the most prescient being Nicholas Carr's 2010 book, *The Shallows: What the Internet is Doing to Our Brains*, in which he discusses how as the plasticity of our brains adapts itself at the biological level to how we use the Internet and other virtual devices, we are rapidly losing the capacities for deep reading and deep concentration due to how we are continually distracted as we jump from one web page or hyperlink to another. Referencing the great media guru from the 1960s, Marshall McLuhan, Carr proceeds to point out how technologies like the Internet are not just passive channels of information. They not only supply the stuff of thought, they also shape the process of thought itself. And what the Internet and other digital devices appear to be doing to many people, according to Carr, is chipping away at their capacities for concentration and contemplation. That is, our minds are becoming ever more conditioned to take in information the way the digital world distributes it—in a swiftly moving stream of pieces of information rather than like a scuba diver who permits himself to become deeply immersed in a sea of words and thoughts.

Furthermore, when we go online, we enter an environment that promotes cursory reading, hurried and distracted thinking, and superficial learning as the Internet's cacophony of stimuli short-circuits both our conscious and our unconscious thoughts; thus preventing our minds from thinking more deeply and creatively. In addition, writes Carr, this is not just a matter of psychological conditioning. For the Internet is in fact a carefully designed interruption system, a machine geared for diverting and dividing attention, that has actual neurological consequences for our entirely malleable brains.

Obviously, whether or not one is in complete agreement with Carr, there has to be the concern that such a distracted, fragmented attention might in fact be occurring in our young people, whose brains are much more malleable than our own, as they spend increasing amounts of time online or focusing on the latest digital device. A 2010 *New York Times* article, "Growing Up Digital, Wired for Distraction," focuses on this issue by delineating how researchers say that the lure of digital technologies, while affecting adults, is particularly powerful for young people, the risk being that developing brains can become more easily habituated than adult brains to constantly switching tasks—and less able to sustain attention. The article quotes Michael Rich, an associate professor at Harvard Medical School and executive director of the Center on Media and Child Health in Boston, who explains that young people's brains are rewarded for not staying on task but for jumping to the next thing. Hence, the worry is that we're raising a generation of children in front of digital screens whose brains are inevitably going to be wired differently.

At the same time, contrary to the warnings of people like Nicholas Carr or Michael Rich, schools across the country are obviously intensifying their efforts to use digital technologies in the classroom, seeing them as a way to better motivate students while giving them essential skills. Increasingly, classrooms are equipping themselves with the Internet or the latest digital technologies and mobile devices so they can attempt to teach students on their own technological territory, so to speak; a process that can obviously produce many positive benefits as far as creative thinking and learning and collaboration with others while doing so are concerned.

Yet, at the same time, since Nicholas Carr's book and the revealing *New York Times article*, there have been any number of similar books and articles concerning how digital technologies are affecting young peoples' attention spans and ability to concentrate, and this obviously is a subject that needs to be studied in increasing depth if our present digital age is in fact creating a harmful, distracted awareness in young people. However, returning to the subject of this particular work, how young people might become more creative learners in preparation for entrance into our present age of high-speed transfer of knowledge and information, there seems to have been scant attention paid to the subject of how digital technologies might actually be affecting students' capacity for creative thinking and learning, the question being what specific effects a distracted awareness might have upon this ever–more important ability.

Clifford Nass, a Stanford University professor in communication and author of the book *The Man Who Lied to His Laptop: What Machines Teach Us about Human Relationships*, has extensively studied how multitasking tends to sap focus; his studies demonstrating how chronic multitaskers are often unable to focus on one thing, even when they are required to do so. Hence, Nass's research has convinced him that such divided attention spans affect creativity because, as he puts it, "Creativity is hard work. It's focus. Really struggling with a thought, rather than lying back and letting it just appear."

Even more to the point, learning expert Annie Murphy Paul, in an article that appeared this past May in *Slate* online, "The New Marshmallow Test: Students Can't Resist Multitasking," writes of how evidence from psychology, cognitive science, and neuroscience suggests that when students are distracted by multitasking while doing their schoolwork, their learning is far spottier and shallower than if the work has their full attention. That is, they tend to understand and remember less, and even more importantly in terms of the subject of this book, creative learning for the information age, *they have greater difficulty transferring their learning to new contexts.* This means that it may become more difficult for them to recognize certain relationships or connections they may have apprehended in one area of learning in another.

Consequently, if the attention spans of students are growing increasingly distracted as they enter our present digital world, with all its new devices and possibilities for multitasking, and if this distracted awareness is becoming an impediment to taking creative ways of connecting knowledge and information that they have developed in one subject area and transferring those to another area, then it would seem that this might easily have a profound effect on young people's capacity for more creative learning in an age that will increasingly demand it of them.

As was discussed earlier in this work, the ability to identify various connections and relationships that students might have apprehended in one particular area of learning in order to develop their own creative paths toward absorbing it, and then recognize those same relationships in another area is going to fundamentally enhance their ability to think and learn creatively. This means that when young learners can identify structural similarities that exist within different areas of learning, they will be able to more easily relate facts, ideas, and knowledge in new areas of learning in which they are engaged.

On the other hand, if their apprehension of a certain area of learning is shallower because that learning does not command their complete attention, then it would appear to be inevitable that it is going to be not only more difficult for them to recognize all the relevant connections within it, but at the same time, it will become even harder for them to recognize similar relationships to which they might give themselves access in a different area of learning. As a result, as these same young people grow toward adulthood, this more superficial awareness of different areas of human endeavor engendered by an inability to recognize similar relationships that exist within different areas might well lessen their capacity for perceiving different areas of endeavor more creatively in their adult or professional lives, particularly those which might have a distinct relationship to one another.

Therefore, one of the important issues that seemingly needs to be studied in connection with a distracted awareness that might be developing in young people due to the amount of time they spend absorbed in their various digital devices or else involving themselves in the different forms of multitasking in which they are presently engaged is how this might be affecting their ability to learn creatively amidst an ever-increasing number of new digital devices that make multitasking not only easier, but also ever more attractive.

David Meyer, a psychology professor at the University of Michigan who has studied the effects of divided attention on learning, has pointed to how the brain simply cannot do two complex tasks at the same time. Rather it can only focus on two tasks simultaneously if both are very simple and they don't compete with each other for the same mental resources. In other words, washing dishes while listening to the news on cable television is alright, but listening to a lecture while texting is not.

Obviously, if distracted awareness is being engendered in young people as a result of how much they habitually multitask while performing two complex tasks, such as reading a book while being on Facebook, this does not auger well for their future ability to recognize significant relationships in one particular area of learning before recognizing similar connections in a different area—different tasks that are not only highly complex, but at the same time require the same mental capacity, that of apprehending similar significant relationships in two different areas that might not be initially obvious. As a result of this, one can easily see that it could become more difficult for young learners to recognize structural similarities between new areas of learning and previous ones in a way that allows them to recognize relationships and connections in those new areas and hence become more creative in attempting to absorb them in new, original ways.

Likewise, it becomes easy to see how young students' developing a distracted, shallow awareness could affect other abilities referred to in this work—abilities that are keys to creative thinking and learning, all of them being complex and drawing on the same mental resources. Once again, these are such things as the ability to distinguish between knowledge and information that exists in isolation and that which can be related to other knowledge and information, the ability to identify different relationships that might be occurring between seemingly disparate pieces of information, and the ability to connect whole different areas of learning to each other.

Therefore, if a distracted awareness is being engendered in young people today by all of the many digital devices that so often consume their attention, in particular by all of the multitasking in which they are engaged, issues that are being taken ever more seriously by any number of learning theorists and educators, then it may not just be the length of their attention spans that are fundamentally at risk. It could also be their capacity for creative thinking and learning.

In a 2006 study that was published in the *Proceedings of the National Academy of Sciences*, Russell Poldrack of the University of Texas–Austin and two colleagues asked participants to engage in a learning activity on a computer while also carrying out a second task, counting musical tones that sounded while they worked. Subjects who performed both tasks simultaneously initially appeared to learn just as well as subjects who did the first task by itself. But upon further study, the former group was less able to extend and extrapolate their new knowledge to novel situations. In addition, brain scans taken during the experiment revealed that different regions of the brain were active under the two conditions, indicating that the brain engages in a different form of memory when forced to pay attention to two streams of information at once. This suggests, the scientists who conducted the experiment wrote, that "even if distraction does not decrease the overall level of learning, it can result in the acquisition of knowledge that can be applied less flexibly in new situations."

Obviously, this dynamic can have a potentially negative effect on young students' capacities for creative thinking and learning. At the same time, however, it might likewise have the same negative effect on their initiative to learn. Returning to the previously mentioned 2009 study by researchers from different departments of psychology concerning embodied and disembodied learning, particularly relevant here may be the researchers' contention that for learning to occur in which students are fully submerged in whatever subject matter they are apprehending, they necessarily need to incorporate the more fixed aspects of the knowledge they are attempting to assimilate into their own flexible, goal-driven approaches. Otherwise, young students who are attempting to absorb the more fixed aspects of certain basic skills they are trying to learn may in fact lose a certain amount of initiative to do so when they aren't able to incorporate these fixed aspects into novel approaches they might have created that allow them to reconfigure their learning in a manner that makes the most sense to them—thus allowing them the greatest amount of flexibility while being engaged in it.

In other words, it may be entirely possible that if a distracted awareness that is being created in young people vis-à-vis multitasking and their increasing connection to the digital world results in a lack of flexibility in transferring what they might have learned while apprehending certain aspects of one subject area to another one, this process might likewise be making it more difficult for them to connect the more fixed aspects of certain subject matters to various aspects of their own personal experience (i.e., curiosities, interests, strength of impressions), inevitably leading toward a dulling of their initiative to learn.

During the time our school in Evanston was in existence, there were of course a number of students who spent a great deal of time on one of the school computers, or else when away from school, playing computer games at home. In the case of several of these students, the single biggest common denominator tended to not necessarily be a lack of focus when they needed to concentrate on something, but on their initiative to follow through on various learning situations when they were away from the computer due to the very fact that they were often unable to imagine these situations in unique ways that had meaning to them.

Hence, even though we may not have fully realized it at the time in which the new digital age was just spawning and working its way through our school, it seems entirely possible that, due to a distracted awareness being created in students by the time they spent in the virtual world, the initiative to learn was already being compromised in some students by their inability to think outside the box, so to speak, in making learning situations and subject matter more meaningful to them. Of course, now that the digital age has expanded exponentially from the time our school was in existence, largely through the emergence of mobile devices, this same effect in many schools, if it indeed exists, must almost certainly have become heightened to a significant degree.

Once again, in the words of Clifford Nass, creativity means the hard work of focusing, as does the initiative to take one's creative ideas and make something of them. If a distracted awareness facilitated by the various digital devices that are available to young people today is indeed affecting both their capacity for creative thought and their initiative to follow through with any creative ideas that they might have, then there is in fact a huge irony lurking at the center of this new digital world that we have now entered. This is simply that as creativity and initiative become ever more important in our current age of high-speed information exchange and rapidly changing knowledge, these very attributes may be in the process of being significantly diluted inside young people by the very devices that make communication in this new age possible.

Our new digital age, and how it might be creating a distracted awareness in young people, may also be affecting their ability to actually absorb new knowledge and information. Recent imaging studies of people have found that major sections of the brain become surprisingly active during downtime; these studies suggesting to researchers that periods of rest are critical in allowing the brain to absorb information or make connections between different ideas that have been recently assimilated. Yet obviously, as young people today spend more and more time with their digital devices, they allow themselves increasingly less downtime as they spend time online or staring into the plastic screens of their iPhone or iPad. Hence, they may well be not allowing their brains the time needed to creatively make connections between different bits of information that they have recently learned.

A 2007 study, conducted by John Kounios, professor of Psychology at Drexel University and Mark Jung-Beeman of Northwestern University, revealed a distinct pattern of brain activity, even at rest, in those people who tend to solve problems with creative insight. That is, the researchers' study showed that the right hemisphere of the brain, which is involved in connecting loose or remote associations between the different elements of a problem—a process that is understood to be an important component of creative thought—occurred even in a resting state in those with a tendency to solve problems with a greater degree of creative insight. This finding obviously suggests that the unique thinking of creative individuals happens even while they are daydreaming or when their minds are at rest.

Therefore, if young people do indeed need to rest their minds in this manner in order to make significant creative connections with their learning, the same ones alluded to throughout this work, and their awareness is being increasingly distracted in the manner in which those such as Nicholas Carr argue it is for all of us, then it would appear obvious that we as educators and parents need to find a way to begin weaning our young people from the rate at which they use their virtual devices, particularly in habitual, non-productive ways. This is true if they are indeed going to be able to focus on becoming more creative thinkers in preparation for the age of high-speed information they are about to enter.

David Anderson, a professor of psychology at the University of Massachusetts at Amherst, who has done research showing that children are not as harmed by TV viewing as some researchers have suggested, believes that young, developing brains are becoming ever more habituated to distraction by the type of multitasking that highly stimulating computers and phones are engendering in them. Hence, he says, young people develop an ever-increasing need for the sort of distracted stimulation that their digital devices are creating in them simply because as they grow up simultaneously processing multiple devices, that's exactly the mode they're going to fall into when put in that particular environment.

If researchers such as David Anderson, and those who were part of the 2007 study involving a resting brain and creativity are correct, young people may be losing the focus necessary for creative apprehension of various learning areas at the same time that, because their brains aren't experiencing enough downtime away from their digital devices, they aren't providing themselves with the type of mental space that will allow them to make important connections and perceive significant relationships. The result of the confluence of these two factors potentially is that mental activity develops that is, at one and the same time, less focused yet also less creative.

As young people enter our age of high-speed information and rapidly changing knowledge, they are going to need to learn how to apprehend various areas of human endeavor more creatively by developing a more acute focus on areas of knowledge that are evolving at an increasingly rapid rate at the same time that they are going to need to imagine those same areas in as broad a context as possible. Yet ironically, as has been suggested in the previous chapter, the very digital devices, themselves responsible for the rate at which knowledge and information are communicated in our present age while it likewise rapidly changes, may be at the same time engendering the very type of mental activity in our young people that will in the long run actually make it more difficult for them to develop a more expansive, creative approach toward various problems and situations necessary for success in this new information age.

IDEAS FOR REFLECTION

How might young people employ the increasing array of digital devices that have now entered their world in a manner that allows them to become more creative and expansive with their learning, but at the same time doesn't create a distracted awareness that actually hinders creative, expansive thinking? This, it would seem, is going to become a significant question that is going to remain with us far down the road, particularly as researchers, educators, and parents are able to more closely observe the effects that the digital world is having on children's brains, attention spans, and creative thought processes.

Certain researchers, such as Cathy Davidson in her book *Now You See It*, defend the new, distracted awareness being engendered in young people, as do many digital natives of the millennial generation who are proud of their increasing ability to multitask, on the grounds that a distracted awareness is actually an awakening—a new, twenty-first century way of paying attention that is more suitable to our current digital age. Yet according to other experts such as learning theorist Annie Murphy Paul or researcher Clifford Nass, Davidson and others with a similar apprehension of the nature of attention in this new age tend to ignore the inflexible and near-universal limits of our working memory that allow us to hold only a few items of information in our awareness at any one time, while also ignoring the fact that human cognition is ill-suited for attending to multiple streams of information and for simultaneously performing multiple tasks.

Needless to say, this particular debate concerning the digital world and attention, particularly in terms of the cognitive development and learning of those in their formative years, is going to take place for many years to come. Yet, in terms of the subject of this book, how young people might learn more creatively in preparation for their entrance into an age of high-speed information transfer that is going to increasingly demand such learning of them, it would appear to be highly important that the capacity for the type of relational thinking that is able to seamlessly connect seemingly disparate pieces of information be carefully studied in relation to the distracted awareness that is being engendered in our young people through multitasking and all of the digital devices that have presently flooded the world of the young.

For if the very devices that are allowing young people to become more creative, expansive, and collaborative with their learning are at the same time engendering in them a lessening of the very cognitive processes that will allow them to think more creatively and expansively in collaboration with others, then young learners may soon be entering a world where the latest technologies might be presenting them with greater opportunities for success while, at the same time, actually impeding their capacity to become fully successful while using those same technologies. That would indeed be a shame.

Chapter Ten

The Future of Schooling

There has been significant attention drawn recently toward a number of the issues explored in this book. That is, educators are growing ever more aware that young learners in their formative years are going to need to learn how to think more creatively and how to collaborate with others in doing so as they approach adulthood in the current information age and global marketplace. Yet the more open-ended question remains of how to structure the modern classroom as a means of facilitating these two increasingly important capacities. For it would seem that the abilities to approach areas of learning more inventively and to collaborate best with others in order to engender this more innovative learning are not going to occur unless they are proceeded by the sort of fundamental structural changes that make them possible. That is, these capacities will not develop simply because teachers focus more directly on how to teach them to students when what is really needed is a much more expansive approach to learning in general in which new models are imagined.

If we remain with the traditional model of education, in which the teacher controls, in one way or another, the flow of information and knowledge to the learner, and in which the learner's abilities are primarily judged by how competently he assimilates a predetermined curriculum based on core standards that he has had no hand in creating, there will be little chance that students will be educated to learn more creatively. For both of these things would appear to be in direct contradiction to how a teacher might assist young people to think more expansively as they learn so that they are able to instinctively perceive relations and patterns within a particular subject matter.

A much better model is one in which the primary role of the teacher becomes one of connecting students with skills, information, knowledge, and experts, as well as the larger world outside the classroom door, in a way that allows those students to cease viewing subject matter as being something fixed and static. Rather, this better model permits students to view different areas of learning as being flexible, malleable, and organic so that they might take them in whichever direction their creative instincts lead.

To this end, it would appear that several issues need to be addressed. The first is a closer examination is needed of how creative thinking and learning actually occur so that new models can be built upon this realization. One approach, alluded to earlier in this work, is that in which students approach knowledge and information from the inside out in order to make inventive connections as they learn. Needless to say, predetermined core curricula work entirely against this idea simply because, when knowledge and information are given to students in advance at the beginning of lessons, they lose the opportunity to make their own creative connections as they learn.

Secondly, the issue of student and teacher accountability needs to be reexamined. For if educators continue to rely on empirical standards such as standardized test scores to evaluate the learning of students, they will lose the opportunity to create a truer, more organic accountability—one that holds students accountable for not just assimilating specific knowledge and information, but also for developing their own creative paths toward it in preparation for thinking more creatively when they enter a modern information age that will increasingly demand it of them.

Thirdly, educators will need to focus on giving students a new set of skills that will more effectively prepare them for the world they are about to inherit. Some of these new skills, those alluded to earlier, are the ability to perceive relationships and patterns both within and between different areas of knowledge; the ability to distinguish between facts and information that exist in isolation and those that can be related; the ability to distinguish between information and knowledge that must be learned and that which can simply be retrieved. And most importantly, students will need to acquire the capacity to develop unique learning progressions toward various subject matter through the use of one's creative instincts.

We have now entered a new age that is just as profound, in its own right, as the industrial age that came into existence during the late nineteenth and early twentieth centuries. This of course is the age of immediate access to information and the age of horizontal relations that now exist in business, commerce, technology, and the arts. So, in a manner similar to how John Dewey indicated twentieth century schools needed to reflect relations in the industrial age, twenty-first-century schools need to reflect relations in the current information age. Otherwise, the mind-set of students in their formative years and the world they are inheriting will continue to be out of synch, much to the students' disadvantage.

Among the recommendations of the New Commission on the Skills of the American Workforce in *Tough Choices or Tough Times* was that of moving toward a more performance-based approach to evaluating student learning, an approach in which students would know in advance specifically which information, knowledge, or set of skills was important for them to be responsible for acquiring so that they could then move toward these at their own pace, with performance evaluations, rather than statistical measures, determining whether or not they had succeeded.

In other words, after students had acquired the knowledge and skills that were important for them to absorb before they moved to a more advanced level of learning, whether it be high school, vocational school, or a traditional four-year college, they could move to that next level simply by demonstrating their competence on performance evaluations designed to determine whether or not they had actually acquired the necessary skills and knowledge. At the same time, the Commission recommended that these performance-based evaluations begin to replace the typical standardized tests in which, because each question has only one correct answer, creative thinking and initiative are inevitably stifled.

In addition, the Commission alluded to the fact that one of the striking contrasts between the American system of education and those of other countries who appeared to be more successful in educating their young people was that American students thought of themselves as putting in time at different levels of the system (i.e., elementary, middle school, secondary school), whereas students in those more successful countries thought of themselves as studying for performance-based evaluations that actually opened doors for them. In other words, there tends to be more of a direct connection between performance-based measures and student initiative than there is between empirical testing and students' motivation to learn.

Although this blueprint has unfortunately been largely ignored by both the American public and the current educational bureaucracy, the idea contained within it of evaluating learning by focusing on actual demonstrations by students that they have learned what is necessary before they are taught at a more advanced level, rather than being continually subjected to empirical test scores, is an essentially sound and important one. In particular, what may be most significant about the plan is that it does not allow empirical testing to stifle creativity and initiative by narrowing curricula to produce certain scores, and likewise does not permit such testing to effectively shove those personal dynamics and developmental concerns that are an important part of creative learning onto the back burner, so to speak.

Yet, there is a step even further down the road that, it would appear, needs to be taken in order to more profoundly prevent these negative trends from occurring. This would be to simply give students a full hand in negotiating individual plans for learning with their teachers, those for which they are willing to be accountable, rather than continuing to subject those students to curricula that are largely predetermined, and for which student learning is evaluated largely through the use of a results-driven measure.

In other words, if educators wish for more creative learning to take place in their students, then it is time for those educators to finally admit that predetermined subject matter and national core standards that students themselves have had no real hand in creating, and empirical testing whose standards the students have had no genuine say in determining, are unfortunate roadblocks that are effectively standing in the way. Therefore, these roadblocks need to be gotten rid of in favor of negotiated curricula and performance-based standards that students would agree to meet simply because they themselves have had a significant hand in designing them.

In addition, if students are to be given this greater degree of latitude with their learning, that which stimulates their creative instincts, they must, regardless of their age, be allowed to move freely around their classroom during the course of a school day, rather than be confined, for a significant part of it, to a desk or table. For, as has been elucidated in earlier chapters, if young people are not able to move freely around their particular learning environment, it is hard to see how they could possibly develop the sort of initiative that will allow them to connect what is transpiring inside them to the objects of their learning. Immobility while one learns leads inevitably toward adherence to someone else's authority in determining the path that one follows in pursing various subject matter; and this adherence to unnatural adult authority then makes it extremely difficult, if not impossible, to fuse initiative with accountability so that the inner lives of students will become more energized and more creative in ways alluded to in earlier chapters of this book.

At the same time, if the creative thinking of children is not to be unnecessarily stifled by the particular environment in which they learn, it seems almost imperative that schools and classrooms become more fully connected to the surrounding community, particularly the world of professional expertise, that exists outside the schoolhouse door. Although obviously many interesting, stimulating lessons and learning experiences take place every day in classrooms throughout the country, nothing would stimulate young people's impressions, curiosities, and creative instincts more than the laboratories of scientists and medical researchers, the busy offices of lawyers or investors, the studios of artists and musicians, the press rooms of newspapers, or working shops and businesses representing all manner of interesting endeavors.

This would be true particularly when what occurs at these workplaces is significantly connected to what young people learn in their classrooms on a daily basis. For then the learning that takes place there could be made to come more fully alive simply because students are experiencing it in a much broader context, one that connects them to the world that they themselves understand they will one day be entering. In fact, consistent, ongoing connections between the world of professional expertise and classroom learning would almost certainly facilitate both creative learning and initiative in young students more fully than anything that one could possibly imagine.

In addition, if academic learning is more fully connected to the world outside of school, relations with those from whom students might learn and with the objects of that learning themselves would necessarily become more meaningful and more genuine. At the same time, students would be less likely to perceive what they learn in school as having a fixed endpoint by which they are often unnecessarily stifled.

Finally, as more and more young people spend a significant amount of time each day with their digital devices, educators and parents, as well as educational researches, need to keep close watch on how that digital world might be affecting those young people's cognition in relation to their capacity to think and learn creatively so that their creative instincts don't become dulled by the very tools that are giving them a greater opportunity to think and learn more expansively. This is particularly needed in a world in which so much knowledge and information is now available to them at the same time that they are able to more fully collaborate with others in accessing it.

Otherwise, it seems, our young people may become like astronomers using a new, special telescope that allows them to see more deeply into the far reaches of the universe while, at the same time, this same telescope is having a deleterious effect on the health of their eyes to the point where it affects their vision. That would be deeply unfortunate.

IDEAS FOR REFLECTION

The time has now come to move our national conversation on education away from discussions that focus solely on how to engender better test scores, or how long the school day or school year should be, or even how to attract more qualified people to the teaching profession, to a discussion of how to implement real structural changes that will, in the end, make a genuine difference in addressing the issue of how more creative learning can be engendered in young learners in an age of high-speed information that will increasingly demand it of them. Once again, these changes should include the following:

• placing the issue of what transpires inside children as they learn—their actual personal dynamics—at the very forefront in allowing them a greater hand in developing their own curricula, subject matter, and learning progressions;

- replacing purely empirical measures of learning such as standardized test scores and grades with performance-based standards that the students themselves have had a significant hand in developing;
- replacing predetermined curricula and core standards with negotiated learning plans that students have played an important role in developing, and that integrally tie accountability to initiative in ways that allow young people's learning to become more creative and more interesting to them;
- giving young people the latitude to move freely around their classroom as they learn as a basic right that they should necessarily enjoy; and finally,
- connecting classroom learning, on an ongoing, regular basis, to the world of professional expertise that exists outside the classroom door, with teachers taking on the role of conduits working to partner students with experts from the world of adult work.

These are all things that can actually be accomplished if educational bureaucrats, principals, and classroom teachers are willing to give up the false notion that for young people's learning to be meaningful, it must necessarily be predetermined by adults before it takes place. In other words, one dynamic that might be actually standing in the way of young students' learning more creatively in preparation for the world they are about to inherit is our false belief, which we cling to, that unless a young person's learning is determined in advance of his coming to it, it will inevitably grow random and chaotic.

That is, we are not able to trust that by following children's enthusiasms, curiosities, and personal needs, we will be able to carve out an approach to their learning, with their participation, that allows them to be both more effective and more creative while they learn simply because it originates with what is transpiring inside them. If we are to genuinely change our schools so that young people are more prepared for the world they are about to inherit, we must begin that period of trust.

Bibliography

Anderson, Porter. *Study: Multitasking is Counterproductive.* CNN.com. August 7, 2001.

Bornstein, David. *How to Change the World: Social Entrepreneurs and the Power of New Ideas.* New York: Oxford University Press, 2004.

Boss, Suzie, and Krauss, Jane. *Reinventing Project-Based Learning: Your Field Guide to Real-World Projects in the Digital Age.* Eugene, OR: International Society for Technology in Education, 2007.

Carlsson-Paige, Nancy. *Taking Back Childhood: A Proven Roadmap for Raising Confident, Creative, Compassionate Kids.* New York: Hudson Street Press, 2008.

Carr, Nicholas. *The Shallows: What the Internet is Doing to Our Brains.* New York: W. W. Norton & Company, Inc., 2011, 2010.

Cifuentes, L. S., and Yu-Chih, Doris. (2001) "Teaching and Learning Online: A Collaboration Between U.S. and Taiwanese Students." *Journal of Research on Computing in Education,* 33, no. 4 (Summer 2001): 456.

Csikszentmihalyi, Mihaly. *Flow: The Psychology of Optimal Experience.* New York: Harper and Row, 1990.

Common Core Standards Initiative, 2012.

Davidson, Cathy. *Now You See It: How the Brain Science of Attention Will Transform the Way We Live, Work, and Learn.* New York: Viking Press, 2011.

Deci, E. L., R. Koestner, and R. M. Ryan. "A Meta-Analytic Review of Experiments Examining the Effects of Extrinsic Rewards on Intrinsic Motivation." *Psychological Bulletin* 125, no. 6 (1999): 627–68.

Dennison, George. *The Lives of Children.* Reading, MA: Addison-Wesley Publishing Company, Inc., 1969.

Dewey, John. *The Child and the Curriculum.* London: The University of Chicago Press, 1902.

Doolittle, Emilie. "How Fortune 100 Companies are Flattening Hierarchies through Enterprise Social." Enterprise Social Network Blog. March 8, 2012.

Drake, Susan M., and Burns, Rebecca C. "Meeting Standards Through Integrated Curriculum." ASCD (Association for Supervision and Curriculum Development) website. March 15, 2013.

Dreyfus, Hubert L. *On the Internet (Thinking in Action).* New York: Routledge, 2001.

Eby, Douglas. "The Complexity of the Creative Personality." psychcentral.com. February 3, 2011.

Eby, Douglas. "Divided Attention Spans and Creativity." talentdevelop.com/4183.

Frampton, Jez. *5 Ways to Build Brands in the Post-Digital World.* www.fastcocreate.com.

Friedman, Thomas L. *The World Is Flat: A Brief History of the Twenty-First Century.* New York: Farrar, Straus, and Giroux, 2005.

Friedman, Thomas L., and Michael Mandelbaum. *How America Fell Behind in the World It Invented and How We Can Come Back.* New York: Picador, 2011.

Gardner, Howard. *Frames of Mind: The Theory of Multiple Intelligences.* New York: Basic Books, 1983.

Gardner, Howard. *The Unschooled Mind: How Children Think and How Schools Should Teach.* New York: Basic Books, 1991.

Gardner, Howard. *Creating Minds: An Anatomy of Creativity.* New York: Basic Books, 1993.

Gatto, John Taylor. *Dumbing Us Down.* Gabriola Island, BC: New Society Publishers, 1992.

Gatto, John Taylor. *Weapons of Mass Instruction.* Gabriola Island, BC: New Society Publishers, 2009.

Gray, Peter. "Freedom to Learn," *Psychology Today.* February 21, 2013.

Hanson, David M. *Instructor's Guide to Process-Oriented Guided-Inquiry Learning.* Lysle, IL: Pacific Crest, 2006.

Harris, Karen, and Pressley, Michael. "The Nature of Cognitive Strategy Instruction: Interactive Strategy Construction." *Exceptional Children* 57, no. 5 (1991).

Hockenberry, Alison Craiglow. "In Our New Sputnik Moment, the Solutions are Down on the Ground." Huffingtonpost.com. May 26, 2011.

"Horizontal Collaboration in the Healthcare Supply Chain." *Deutsche Post DHL*—The Mail and Logistics Group.

Jerome, Annamaria, and Patricia M. Barbetta. "The Effect of Active Student Responding during Computer-Assisted Instruction on Social Studies Learning by Students with Learning Disabilities." *Journal of Special Education Technology* 20, no. 3. (2005).

Jia, Lile, Edward R. Hirt, and Samuel C. Karpen. "Lessons from a Faraway Land: The Effect of Spatial Distance on Creative Cognition." *Journal of Experimental Social Psychology* 45, no. 5 (September 2009).

Kelly, Melissa. "Integrating Curriculum: Importance of Curriculum Integration." About.com, Secondary Education.

Lehman, Rosemary. "The Role of Emotion in Creating Instructor and Leaner Presence in the Distance Education Experience." *Journal of Cognitive Affective Learning* (Spring 2006).

McNeil, Linda. *Contradictions of School Reform: Educational Costs of Standardized Testing.* New York: Routledge, 2000.

Michie, Gregory. *Holler If You Hear Me: The Education of a Teacher and His Students,* 2nd ed. New York: Teachers College Press, 2009.

Miller, Sadker David, and Karen R. Zittleman. *Teacher, Schools, and Society: A Brief Introduction to Education.* Columbus, OH: McGraw-Hill Higher Education, 2006.

Mone, Gregory. "Better Nature." *Discover* (April 2013).

Montessori, Maria. *The Absorbent Mind.* New York: Holt, Rinehart, and Winston, Inc., 1967.

Moore, Karl, and Hill, Kyle. "The Decline but Not Fall of Hierarchy: What Young People Really Want." *Forbes.com.* www.forbes.com/sites/karlmoore. June 14, 2011.

National Center on Education and the Economy. *Tough Choices or Tough Times.* San Francisco: Jossey-Bass, 2007.

Pacific Policy Research Center. *21st Century Skills for Students and Teachers.* Honolulu: Kamehamehu Schools Research and Evaluation Division. 2010.

Paul, Annie Murphy. "The New Marshmallow Test: Student's Can't Resist Multitasking." Slate.com. May 3, 2013.

Paul, Annie Murphy. "Who's Afraid of Digital Natives?" Slate.com. August 2011.

"Partnering for Excellence: STEM Partnership Innovations." Opportunityequation.org.

Piaget, Jean, and Barbel Inhelder. *The Psychology of the Child.* Translated by Helen Weaver. New York: Basic Books, 1969.

Pink, Daniel. *A Whole New Mind: Moving from the Information Age to the Conceptual Age.* New York: Penguin Group, 2005.

Poldrack, Russell. *Proceeding of the National Academy of Sciences,* 2006 study.

Postman, Neil. *The Disappearance of Childhood.* New York: Vintage Books, 1982.

Richland, Lindsey E. *Analogy and Classroom Mathematics Learning.* In *Developmental Cognitive Science Goes to School* edited by N. L. Stein and S. Raudenbush.. New York: Lawrence Erlbaum Associates, 2010.

Richtel, Matt. "Growing Up Digital, Wired for Distraction." *New York Times.* November 21, 2010.

Rosenthal, Robert, and Lenore Jacobson. *Pygmalion in the Classroom: Teacher Expectation and Pupil's Intellectual Development.* New York: Irvington Publishers, 1992.

Sadker, David Miller, and Karen R. Zittleman. *Teachers, Schools, and Society: A Brief Introduction to Education.* New York: McGraw-Hill Higher Education, 2006.

Savoia, Alberto, and Patrick Copeland. *Entrepreneurial Innovation at Google.* IEEE Computer Society. 2011.

Drexel University. "Brain Activity Differs for Creative and Noncreative Thinkers." Science-Daily. October 29, 2007.

Shapiro, Oren, and Nira Lieberman. "An Easy Way to Increase Creativity." *Scientific American,* July 21, 2009.

Sheldrake, Rupert. *A New Science of Life: The Hypothesis of Formative Causation.* Los Angeles, CA: J. P. Tarcher, 1981.

Strauss, Valerie. "Eight Problems with Common Core Standards." *Washington Post,* August 21, 2012.

Thompson, Scott. "How Do Organic Organizational Structures Affect External Hierarchical Organizational Structures?" Small Business—Chron.com.

Wagner, Tony. *The Global Achievement Gap: Why Even the Best Schools Don't Teach the New Survival Skills Our Children Need.* New York: Basic Books, 2008.

Wagner, Tony. *Creating Innovators: The Making of Young People Who Will Change the World.* New York: Scribner, 2012.

"What is an Organic Organizational Structure." Wise GEEK. March 18, 2013.

Winkielman, Piotr, Daniel N. McIntosh, and Lindsay Oberman. "Embodied and Disembodied Processing: Learning From and About Typical and Autistic Individuals." *Emotion Review* 1, no. 2 (April 2009): 178–90.

Wu, Yong, and Zhicheng Ma. "Principles and Practices Report on Online Enrichment and Extension for the Gifted and Talented." *Canadian Social Science,* January 1, 2009.

About the Author

From 1991 to 2003, Lyn Lesch was founder and director of The Children's School in Evanston, Illinois, a private, progressive, democratically run school for children six to fourteen years of age. During its existence, the school received widespread attention in both the electronic and print media in Chicago as a unique, innovative approach to education.

Lyn is also the author of three books on education reform, published by Rowman & Littlefield Education. They are: *Our Results-Driven, Testing Culture: How It Adversely Affects Students' Personal Experience* (2007); *How to Prepare Students for the Information Age and Global Marketplace: Creative Learning in Action* (2008); and *Learning Not Schooling: Reimagining the Purpose of Education* (2009).

He can be found on the Web at Center for Educational Purpose, where he blogs and writes about education concerns, and about the effect of modern culture and technology on young people.

CPSIA information can be obtained at www.ICGtesting.com
Printed in the USA
BVOW01*0141130514

353310BV00002B/5/P